WHICH WINE
WHICH FOOD

Jill Cox and Tony Lord

Mitchell Beazley

WHICH WINE
WHICH FOOD

Edited and designed by Mitchell Beazley,
an imprint of Reed Consumer Books Ltd,
Michelin House, 81 Fulham Road, London SW3 6RB
and Auckland, Melbourne, Singapore and Toronto

A CIP catalogue record for this book is available from
the British Library.
ISBN 1 85732 385 8

Editor: Diane Pengelly
Indexer: Ann Barrett
Production: Michelle Thomas
Executive Editor: Anne Ryland

Typeset in M Gill Sans
Produced by Mandarin Offset
Printed and bound in Malaysia

CONTENTS

INTRODUCTION

Not so long ago the following section on appetizers would have been called Hors d'Oeuvres and the suggested wines would have stuck close to a classic but fairly inflexible list of 'acceptable' partners. Dry and light whites such as Muscadet, Sancerre or Pouilly-Fumé were routinely recommended, light reds like Cru Beaujolais or Mâcon Rouge and rosés such as Tavel or Provence.

But today popular food and wine draw their inspiration from much further afield than classic French cuisine. Regional specialities from all over the world have become international fare and part of a much more relaxed and cosmopolitan approach to eating and drinking.

This makes finding exciting food and wine partnerships all the more interesting: the possibilities are – literally – endless.

Partly because of the ever greater freedom of choice, however, and partly because of the enormous range of wines and foods now readily available it is often helpful to have a point of reference when putting together a menu, however informal or otherwise the occasion.

Which Wine Which Food is designed to provide that point of reference. Listing over 650 dishes, with suggested wines to go with each of them, it should help to whet even the most jaded appetite. Whether you are looking for an appropriate partner for the paella or just a new dish to eat with your favourite rosé, it should at the very least give you somewhere exciting to start.

HOW TO USE THIS GUIDE

The first difficulty every cook encounters when planning or organising a meal on any scale is – where to start. The prompt may be the occasion, the season, the size of the party or even what ingredients there are to hand at the time. So in organising a book like this, the first priority has been to make it quick and easy to refer to, whether you are looking for a wine to complement a simple meal, planning an elaborate dinner party or simply looking for inspiration.

One comprehensive index lists by name all the dishes mentioned as well as listing them by main ingredient, in case your Beef Casserole also masquerades as a Pot au Feu, a Ragoût or a Boeuf en Daube.

The second index lists the wines, so, should you be looking for a good excuse to open a Hungarian Tokay, or want to find a selection of Bordeaux-friendly possibilities to complement your favourite claret, the answers are listed here.

The book is organised into ten chapters, beginning with appetizers and ending with desserts. In addition, there are sections on Special Occasions, Picnics, Barbecues and Winter Parties, which suggest general guidelines for the prospective organiser, and The Wine Grapes (pages 120 to 124) is a convenient précis of the aromas and tastes produced by specific varieties. So even if you have only the vaguest idea of the occasion you want to cater for, leafing through a particular section should suggest a selection of appetizing possibilities.

5

APPETIZERS & LIGHT DISHES

Appetizers can range from simple finger foods through first courses to light meals. They can include anything from a bowl of nuts to luxuries like freshly shucked oysters. A glass or two of – usually light – wine can make them that much more enjoyable and help to whet the appetite for what is to come.

In Spain, where the appetizer has been lifted to an art form, bars everywhere serve small dishes called tapas. These can be simple dishes such as a few fresh prawns or rich concoctions like kidneys in sherry.

Many of the dishes suggested below can be expanded or contracted according to the mood: you may wish to serve a few small amuse-gueules ('mouth tantalisers'?) to nibble between cocktails, or lay on a selection of tempting platters to sustain a party at a buffet-style lunch. In either case the suggestions below should provide some food for thought.

Angels on Horseback
Oysters wrapped in bacon and grilled
Choose a fresh dry fino sherry, a dry montilla or a light white wine such as Chilean Sauvignon Blanc

Artichokes, Globe
with Hollandaise
Try a full-bodied California Sauvignon Blanc

with Melted Butter
Good with a light crisp white wine like an Alto Adige from northern Italy or an Australian Riesling

with Vinaigrette
Muscadet de Sèvre et Maine sur lie

Artichokes, Jerusalem

Mornay: onion, ham and cheese sauce
*Best accompanied by a new-wave Italian
Chardonnay*

Salad: with bacon
*Muscadet de Sèvre et Maine sur lie will
suit this*

Asparagus

with Butter
*Needs the crispness of Italy's Verdicchio or
try a chilled fino sherry*

Hollandaise
*This calls for a full-bodied Sauvignon Blanc
from Australia or California*

Vinaigrette
*Try a Galestro, a dry white wine from
Tuscany*

Aubergine Purée

*The rich, smoky, garlicky flavour and smooth
texture of this dipping purée needs a full-
bodied red wine like California's Zinfandel –
or else a Côtes du Rhône*

Avocado Pear

with Crab in a light mayonnaise with dill
*A fragrant, spicy Gewurztraminer from
Alsace or a grapey Muscat makes a good
choice*

with Mayonnaise
*This popular first course needs a crisp Cape
Chenin Blanc or juicy New Zealand
Sauvignon Blanc*

with Prawns
Try a lightly chilled, simple dry white such as an Aligoté from Burgundy

with Raspberry Vinaigrette
A red Loire like a Sancerre Rouge is good with this

Salad with sliced Mozzarella cheese, sliced beef tomatoes and vinaigrette dressing
A crisp dry Italian white, such as a Frascati or Verdicchio, complements this well

Bacon, Lettuce and Tomato Sandwich

Crisp bacon, iceberg lettuce and sliced tomatoes with mayonnaise
Best washed down with a young, fruity Beaujolais or a California Zinfandel

Blinis

Buckwheat pancakes usually served with soured cream and caviar or lumpfish roe
Eat these with a well-chilled glass of Russian or Polish vodka – or a sparkling Saumur

Borekas

Middle-Eastern crisp snack-sized pastry triangles filled with chopped spinach and cheese
Good with a dry Muscat from Alsace

Brandade de Morue

Creamed salt cod, popular in the Languedoc region of southern France
Go for a bone-dry white wine such as Muscadet

Bresaola

Smoked dried beef from Valtellina in

Italy, usually thinly sliced, with olive oil
*Good with one of the region's red wines
such as Valtellina, Grumello or Sassella. Or
try a decent Chianti Classico*

Caesar Salad

Iceberg lettuce with anchovies and
croûtons tossed in egg yolk dressing
with Parmesan cheese
*California Sauvignon Blanc or sparkling
mineral water*

Carpaccio

An Italian dish of raw fillet of beef, thinly
sliced and marinaded
Chianti Classico Riserva

Caviar

Sturgeon roe, served with toast or blinis
(see page 8)
Champagne or chilled Russian vodka

Charcuterie

A selection of continental meats
*Choose a young claret or Chilean Cabernet
Sauvignon*

Chicken Wings

Chinese style: marinaded in ginger, garlic,
soy sauce and sesame oil, deep fried and
sprinkled with toasted sesame seeds
Good with a dry rosé from Provence or Spain

Club Sandwich

America's favourite sandwich – a triple-
decker filled with sliced meat, salad and
mayonnaise
Enjoy with a light California Zinfandel

Croissant

With a savoury filling of cheese and ham

Choose something light and fizzy like a sparkling Saumur or Cava

Croque Madame

Fried sandwich filled with cheese, ham and a poached egg
A glass of Aligoté or Bourgogne Blanc

Croque Monsieur

Fried sandwich with cheese and ham
Best with a glass of beer or simple red wine

Crudités

Strips of raw vegetables served with one or more dips
Something crisp and white such as Vinho Verde, Soave, Frascati, a white Valencia or Penedès

Devils on Horseback

Prunes wrapped in bacon and grilled
Sip a light red such as Valpolicella

Dolmades

Greek speciality of vine leaf parcels stuffed with rice, lamb and herbs
Best with a dry white wine from Greece or Cyprus

Empañadas

Small meat pasties from Spain with sultanas, chopped apricots and other fruit. Larger ones are served as a lunch dish
Choose a Chilean Sauvignon Blanc

Escargots

A French delicacy of snails cooked in their shells with garlic butter
Well matched with a Bourgogne Blanc, Aligoté or a young Pinot Noir

Fiskefars

A Norwegian fish pâté made from puréed cod with creamed shrimps, dill and mild spices
A chilled Scandinavian akvavit is perfect, otherwise an inexpensive dry white wine

Foie Gras

Fattened goose or duck liver, often made into very rich pâté
Sip a lightly chilled Sauternes or Barsac with this: the traditional French accompaniment

Frogs' Legs

Choose a Chablis or the slightly cheaper and more earthy Bourgogne Aligoté

Garlic Bread: see page 90

Gravad Lax

Swedish speciality of fresh salmon marinaded with sugar, salt and dill, thinly sliced and served with a sweet mustard sauce
Traditionally served with a chilled glass of akvavit, but for more conservative tastes try a glass of Muscadet de Sèvre et Maine sur lie

Guacamole

From Mexico, an avocado dip with chilli
Try this with a Mexican lager such as Dos Equis

Ham Mousse

Puréed ham with whipped cream, egg whites and seasonings, set with gelatine and served with croûtons
A delicate first course, good with a young Chardonnay from Australia or New Zealand

Ham Sandwich

Off-the-bone with English mustard
Drink a glass of good ale, an inexpensive claret or a red wine from Navarra

Humus

Middle-Eastern dip made from chickpeas with olive oil, lemon juice, garlic and tahini (sesame seed paste), served with warm pitta bread
This dip benefits from a glass of Gewurztraminer or Hungarian Muscat Ottonel

Jambon d'Ardennes

Belgian ham
This is complemented by a German Spätburgunder or a Gamay grape wine like Beaujolais-Villages

Jamon Serrano

Cured ham from Spain
Good with a Navarran rosé or a young red Rioja

Liver Sausage

A smooth German sausage of minced pork, liver and seasoning, served in slices
A good choice for this is a dry German white wine

Mushrooms on Toast

Served with garlic salt and black pepper
Select a young fruity Beaujolais or Valpolicella

Oysters

Choose Chablis, Sancerre or New Zealand Sauvignon Blanc

Parma Ham

Thinly sliced cured ham from Italy
Best with a young Chianti, Bardolino,
Valpolicella or Nebbiolo d'Alba

with Fruit such as figs or melon
Try a Vernaccia di San Gimignano or a
Chardonnay from Alto Adige or Orvieto Seco

Pâté

Ardennes: rough and meaty
A chunky red like Corbières, Minervois,
Languedoc-Roussillon or Côtes du Rhône

Brussels: smooth and spreadable
Good with a Merlot-based wine

Chicken Liver: sophisticated, flavoured
with garlic and brandy and served with
toast or on toast in Italy as 'Crostini'
This tasty snack or first course is well
matched by a dry Tuscan white like Galestro

Chicken Liver with Truffles
A Cape Chenin Blanc, an Australian Semillon
or Portuguese dry white like Dão are all
good matches

Country: a chunky mixture of liver and
meat with fresh herbs
Drink an Australian Shiraz with this

Duck: usually flavoured with orange or
an orange liqueur
Best with a light cru Beaujolais like Fleurie or
one of the Loire reds: Sancerre, Chinon or
Bourgueil

Pigs' Liver: stronger in flavour than
chicken liver and often rougher-textured
A sturdy pâté, good with a Midi red

Prawn

Cocktail: peeled cooked prawns in
Marie-Rose sauce
A blush wine is a good match

with Mayonnaise
A dry rosé is perfect with this

Rillettes

A coarse-textured terrine made by
roasting pork belly until meltingly tender,
shredding it then packing it into
earthenware pots
*Very rich, so choose a Beaujolais-Villages,
a Chilean Cabernet Sauvignon or a
Gewurztraminer*

Salami

Served thinly sliced as an hors
d'oeuvre
*A light red wine such as Valpolicella or
young Chianti is a good complement for
this dish*

Samosas

Crackly filo pastry triangles filled with
spiced vegetables
*Lager or a light dry white wine such as a
Yugoslav Riesling*

Smoked Salmon

Served with black pepper and lemon
juice
*Choose a Sancerre, Pouilly-Fumé, Chablis or
New Zealand Chardonnay*

Smoked Trout

With horseradish sauce
*Well matched by a California Sauvignon
Blanc – but the partnership is better if you
go easy on the horseradish*

Smørgasbord

A selection of Swedish open sandwiches
with meat, fish and vegetable toppings
*A light and fruity Vinho Verde is a good
choice*

Spring Rolls

Deep-fried crispy pancakes filled with
bamboo shoots, carrot strips and char
sui (roast pork)
*Good with a Chinese wine, fino sherry or a
Bordeaux Blanc*

Tapas

A wide selection of appetizers is served
under this broad Spanish heading: spicy
grilled sweet peppers, for example,
grilled chorizo (spicy Spanish sausage)
Manchego cheese, olives, chicken in
wine, calamares. . . .
*Fino or manzanilla sherry is perfect. Or go
for a dry white wine from Rioja, Penedès,
Valencia or Navarra*

Taramasalata

Greek speciality of smoked cods' roe
paste served with pitta bread
*Needs a wine with crisp acidity – like a New
Zealand Sauvignon Blanc*

EGGS

Eggs are not the easiest ingredient to match with wine, especially when there is a dominance of the egg yolk flavours. Often it is the texture of the dish, the sometimes mouth-coating quality eggs can impart, that makes it difficult – but by no means impossible – to choose a complementary partner.

Benedict

Soft-poached egg served on a roll with sliced ham and topped with Hollandaise sauce

Try a German Kabinett Riesling or an Alsace Riesling. Choose an Australian sparkling wine if served for breakfast, or champagne for a special occasion

Curry

Halved hard-boiled eggs in a lightly curried sauce

Liebfraumilch is gently floral and fruity and a good match

Florentine

Soft-baked eggs placed on a bed of cooked spinach, topped with cheese sauce

The white Tuscan Galestro, Frascati, Soave or Verdicchio are all complementary partners

Fricassée

Hard-boiled eggs with a tarragon and sour cream sauce

This light and herby dish needs a simple wine such as Bulgarian Chardonnay or Hungarian dry white

Mayonnaise

This is rather creamy in texture so keep to an inexpensive dry white wine like a Yugoslav Riesling or Sauvignon Blanc

Omelette

Arnold Bennett: a flat omelette topped with smoked haddock, cream and Parmesan cheese and browned under the grill. Devised especially for the writer Arnold Bennett at the Savoy Hotel in London
This settles well with a bottle of non-vintage champagne

Basquaise: with sweet red peppers and tomatoes
Its attractive blend of flavours goes particularly well with a rosé from Navarra, Rioja or Valencia

Cheese
Choose a New Zealand or Chilean Chardonnay

Fines Herbes
Rather a fragrant omelette, so go for a Bordeaux Blanc or an Alsace dry Muscat

Ham
Good with an Alsace Riesling

Mushroom
A Portuguese dry white wine like a Dão will suit this well, or an English white or even a delicate Australian Riesling

Plain: with plenty of freshly ground black pepper
An English dry white is appropriate here, or a Cape Chenin Blanc

Prawn
Try a crisp Vinho Verde

Seafood
Needs a Frascati

Tomato
Choose a Galestro or Orvieto Seco

Tortilla: a thick cake-like omelette with potatoes and onions, often served in slices as tapas
Good with a chilled fino sherry, a rosado from Navarra or a young unoaked red Rioja

Quails' Eggs

Served hard-boiled and peeled for dipping into seasoned salt
Enjoy these with a Bordeaux or Bergerac Blanc

Quiche

Originating in Lorraine in northern France, a shortcrust tart base with a savoury custard filling
Lorraine: filled with chopped bacon, eggs and cream
A dry Alsace Muscat or Pinot Gris is good

Mushroom: button mushrooms and spring onions
Rich and filling, this goes happily with Cape Chenin Blanc, Chilean Chardonnay or even a much lighter Vinho Verde

Onion
Choose a Pinot Gris to set this off or, if you can find one, an old-style white Rioja

Seafood
Good with an Australian Semillon, Sauvignon or a California Sauvignon Blanc

Scrambled

With smoked salmon
Definitely a sparkling wine. Champagne if possible, otherwise Cava, Spain's champagne-style fizz or sparkling Saumur from the Loire

Soufflé

Cauliflower
A crisp Vinho Verde from Portugal will suit this

Mushroom
Choose a Bordeaux Blanc

Smoked Haddock
Portuguese dry white Dão is a good match

Spinach
Good with a dry and zesty Verdicchio

Tuna
A light red such as Bardolino suits this

SOUPS

Choosing the perfect wine to go with soup is not at all easy. Generally a glass or two of sherry or dry madeira is the best solution, then the wine can be selected to suit the next course. Some soups, though, benefit from the accompaniment of a certain type of wine. These are mainly full-flavoured, rich soups – Oxtail, for example, which needs a robust wine such as a red Côtes du Rhône. Main course soups such as fish or chunky vegetable are also good with wine, when the choice must be made according to the combination of ingredients present.

Avgolemonoo

Greek soup of chicken stock with lemon and egg
A glass of Sercial madeira is a good choice with this, or a lemony Greek or Cypriot dry white wine

Beef Consommé

Traditionally served with amontillado sherry with a further measure added to the soup. On a cold day, a glass of malt whisky goes well

Borscht

Russian beetroot soup
Not the best partner for wine but a dry Szamorodni Hungarian Tokay can be pleasant, or a rosé from Provence

Bouillabaisse

Fish soup with a stew personality
Good accompanied by a New Zealand Sauvignon Blanc

Caldo Verde

A green soup based on shredded cabbage, potatoes and olive oil, famous throughout Portugal
Choose a Vinho Verde or white Dão from Portugal

Carrot Soup

A popular vegetable soup
Very good with a Portuguese rosé

Chicken

Clear Soup: stock made with the carcass, giblets, carrots, celery and onions; strained, reduced, and pasta and chicken strips added
Well partnered by a chilled dry tangy manzanilla sherry

with Lemon and Egg: see Avgolemonoo

Noodle, Chinese Style: shreds of chicken in a clear broth with vegetables and thin noodles
Good with a dry Bordeaux Blanc or Chinese wine

Thick: a velvety cream soup with small chunks of chicken. Traditionally offered by Jewish mothers as panacea for all physical and emotional ills
Try an amontillado sherry or Sercial madeira. One of the new German trocken white wines would be good

Cullen Skink

Scottish soup of smoked haddock and potato
Choose a bottle of Muscadet, Verdicchio or a good Sauvignon Blanc with this

21

Fish Soup

Russet-coloured and rich-tasting, this
soup is made with mixed fish and
shellfish, tomatoes, onion and garlic and
traditionally served with rouille
*Good with a rosé from Provence or a decent
Beaujolais*

French Onion

Sliced onions in a rich brown stock
topped with a cheese-laden croûton
*This has a very heavy flavour of its own, so
settle for an inexpensive southern French
red wine such as Fitou or Corbières or
Languedoc-Roussillon*

Game Soup

*A strong flavour, this needs a light fruity red
wine like a young Chianti*

Gazpacho

Fresh vegetable soup from Andalucía
made from tomatoes, cucumbers, sweet
peppers, olive oil and garlic and served
chilled, sprinkled with chopped hard
boiled egg and croûtons
*A chilled fino sherry or dry montilla is a good
choice, or try a fresh lemony white Rioja*

Hot and Sour Soup

Chinese clear soup with strips of
vegetables and chicken, flavoured with
chilli
*Good with a Chinese wine or a chilled dry
sherry*

Hotch-Potch

Scottish soup of beef, mutton, celeriac
and other root vegetables, dried beans
and fresh peas

Complemented by a dry madeira or a red
Dão from Portugal

Lentil Soup

Warming and filling bowl of puréed
lentils flavoured with belly pork, garlic
and chilli
A meal in itself – so open a bottle of chunky
red wine such as an Australian Shiraz
Cabernet blend

Lobster Bisque

Try a fresh New Zealand Sauvignon Blanc
or South African Chardonnay

Minestrone Soup

Heart-warming Italian soup with haricot
beans, tomatoes, garlic, onions and pasta
served sprinkled with Parmesan cheese
A wholesome dish, great with a simple white
wine like Verdicchio or the dry Galestro from
Tuscany

Mulligatawny Soup

Spicy, Indian-inspired soup of vegetables
flavoured with curry and lemon
Iced lager is best with this

Mushroom Soup

Creamy and velvety, made from
mushrooms and shallots enriched with
cream
Goes well with a dry amontillado sherry or
a New World Chenin Blanc

Mutton Broth

Comforting thick soup with carrots,
onions, celery, leeks and pearl barley
Ideal with a dry oloroso sherry or any young
red wine

New England Fish Chowder

A thickened stew-type soup made from fish and shellfish, sometimes with sweet corn

A middle-priced California or Australian Chardonnay

Oxtail Soup

Wonderfully warming winter soup of chopped oxtails slowly cooked in stock, flavoured with tomato purée and fresh herbs

Try an inexpensive red Côtes du Rhône or red Italian Dolcetto

Pumpkin Soup

A rich, golden, autumn soup

A light red wine such as Beaujolais is a good match

Scotch Broth

Try a nip of whisky or a glass of claret with this robust soup

Tomato Soup

Best with a Languedoc or other southern French red wine

Vegetable Soup

Wholesome and nourishing

A fresh Australian Riesling is a good choice

Vichyssoise

Smooth soup of leeks and potatoes served hot or cold

This traditional French dish is best with an inexpensive white burgundy

Watercress Soup

Light and delicate, served chilled

A dry Alsace Riesling is the perfect choice

Won Ton Soup

Chinese clear soup with pork-filled
dumplings and chopped spring onions
*Choose any simple, inexpensive dry white
wine*

Zuppa di Pesci

Italian fish broth of red mullet, squid,
clams, mussels and lobster with tomato,
fresh herbs and porcini (ceps)
Try a Frascati or Soave

FISH

Fish and shellfish traditionally call for a chilled white wine but in some instances a dry rosé or even a red wine can be better. The occasional dish, mainly Japanese, does not lend itself to wine at all – mainly because of the spices and other flavourings used.

If the dish is a simple one, like grilled haddock or fish and chips, look for a straightforward white wine and save the more expensive classic for a luxury seafood like salmon or lobster.

If the dish is richly sauced, choose a wine with enough natural acidity to cut through the sauce and balance it. Wines like Chablis or New Zealand Sauvignon Blanc do this. Simple dishes need wines that suit both the palate and the pocket.

Anchovies

Jansson's Temptation: a Swedish dish of casseroled potatoes, onions and anchovies
A crisp Verdicchio is a good choice, or a tangy manzanilla sherry

Bouillabaisse

From Marseille in the south of France, a mixed fish and shellfish stew flavoured with herbs, garlic, tomatoes, olive oil and white wine, served with aioli and garlic croûtons
A dry Tavel or Spanish rosé is good with this aromatic and flavourful dish

Calamares

à la Plancha: grilled with garlic

An inexpensive Sauvignon Blanc is best with this mixture of flavours, or a white Penedès

Rellenos: a Spanish dish of baby squid stuffed with breadcrumbs, cured ham, garlic and herbs
Needs a robust wine so try a hearty red from Spain's Ribero del Duero, Rioja or Valdepeñas

Ripeni: an Italian squid dish. The squid is stuffed with breadcrumbs, anchovies, chilli and tuna
Suits a Frascati or Tuscany's Galestro

à la Romana: squid cut into rings, battered then deep fried
Good with a chilled fino sherry or a light wine such as a new-style white Rioja, or Vinho Verde

Ceviche

A Latin-American dish of raw fish marinaded in lime juice, tabasco and olive oil
These flavours do not lend themselves easily to wine but a Muscadet de Sèvre et Maine might suit. Otherwise keep to a dry lager

Cod and Chips

Surprisingly enhanced by a glass of Sauvignon de St-Bris or Soave

Cods' Roe

Grilled and served with chips
Choose a Muscadet de Sèvre et Maine sur lie or a Bordeaux Blanc

Coquilles St-Jacques

Scallops in a creamy sauce served in a scallop shell edged with mashed potato

> Good with a Sancerre or Chablis. A white
> Graves would also match well

Coulibiac

Traditional Russian fish pie with rice and
hard-boiled eggs in a puff pastry
envelope
*Well suited by a Bulgarian Chardonnay, a
dry Tokay Szamorodni or the green-olive
freshness of a chilled fino sherry*

Crab

in Black Bean Sauce
Match this with a dry rosé

Devilled: spiced with tabasco and
mustard and topped with melted cheese
Go for a young, lightly chilled Beaujolais

Dressed
*Delicious with a New Zealand Sauvignon
Blanc*

Mayonnaise
A California blush wine will suit this

Potted
*An inexpensive Chardonnay is a good
partner*

Salad
*Try a Bordeaux Blanc or Australian dry
white wine*

Eels

Jellied: the famous East End of London
dish of chopped cooked eels set in a
savoury jelly
*Quite an oily dish so it needs a dry wine with
a decent brush of acidity such as an Italian
Soave or perhaps Muscadet from northern
France*

Matelote of Eels: from the Loire, a full-flavoured stew of eels, garlic and red wine
This calls for a young claret or a young red Rhône

Smoked with horseradish sauce
Try a glass of chilled fino sherry

Fish Hash

Diced white fish and salmon in a creamy velouté sauce with vegetables
Enhanced by a New Zealand Sauvignon Blanc or Bulgarian Chardonnay

Fishcakes

Flaked white fish mixed with mashed potatoes and herbs, moulded into patties then covered with breadcrumbs and deep fried
An Australian Sauvignon Blanc will fit the bill

Fritto Misto

An Italian assortment of squid, mullet, white fish and prawns coated in seasoned flour and deep fried
Good with a tangy Frascati or, for a luxury version of the dish with sole, an Italian Chardonnay

Gefilte Fish

Jewish dish of white fish, blended with eggs, onion and matzah meal, shaped into patties and fried or poached, then served with a lemon sauce
A difficult dish to match with wine – but try a Muscadet or an Israeli dry white

Haddock

Arbroath Smokies: oak-smoked and ready to eat

29

Try a tangy manzanilla sherry or smoky malt whisky with these small haddocks from Scotland

Finnan: whole haddocks from Findon in Scotland, smoked over oak sawdust
Cries out for a lemony Muscadet or a smoky Islay malt whisky

Florentine: served on freshly cooked spinach topped with a poached egg and cheese sauce
A California Sauvignon Blanc goes well with this full-flavoured dish

Grilled
Good with a full white wine such as an Australian Semillon or Chilean or Argentinian Chardonnay

Kedgeree: see page 31

Smoked and poached in milk
Try a dry wine like Bordeaux Blanc, Bergerac Blanc, or a Portuguese dry white such as Dão

Hake

à la Plancha: grilled with a drizzle of olive oil and seasoning. This is popular all over Spain as merluza
Makes a perfect match with a dry white wine from Rioja, Penedès, Valencia, Rueda or Navarra

à la Romana: cooked in crisp batter
A white Côtes du Rhône or Touraine

Herring

Boulangère: baked in stock with sliced potatoes and onions and flavoured with thyme

This needs the crisp acidity of a Muscadet

in Oatmeal: a Scottish dish of whole
herrings coated in oatmeal and fried
*Inexpensive but nonetheless delicious, this is
complemented by a simple dry white wine
like a Côtes du Roussillon or Gaillac*

Rollmops: herring fillets marinaded in
spiced vinegar and rolled around
chopped onions. Served with dill pickles
*A popular dish but difficult to partner with
wine because of the oiliness. In Scandinavia
rollmops are served with chilled akvavit, in
Germany with Schnapps and in eastern
Europe with vodka*

Soused: cooked in a malt vinegar, onion,
parsley, allspice and bayleaf marinade and
served cold
Strangely delicious with iced lager

Whitebait: see page 42

John Dory

A fish with meaty flesh, baked whole
with herbs
Good with a crisp New Zealand Blanc

Kedgeree

Based on rice, smoked haddock, hard-
boiled eggs and cream. Often associated
with English Edwardian breakfasts but
served today at fork buffets
*With breakfast, Bucks Fizz, but with dinner
try a dry Bergerac Blanc, Muscat, or St-
Véran*

with Curry Sauce
*Needs a light and simple white wine like a
Hungarian or Yugoslav Riesling*

Kippers

Grilled with a knob of butter: a good supper dish
The smoky taste dominates, so choose any inexpensive dry white wine or a glass of whisky

Jugged: this cooking method removes some of the oiliness and smoky taste
Choose a dry white wine like a Bulgarian Sauvignon Blanc

Langoustines: see Prawns, Dublin Bay

Lobster

Boiled: straight from the sea if possible
A fine Sauvignon Blanc, a Chardonnay or a good white burgundy is perfect

Grilled and served with Hollandaise sauce
This calls for a full-bodied white wine like a New World Chardonnay

Salad: escalopes of lobster on a bed of curly lettuce dressed with a dill vinaigrette
An excellent choice is a Chilean or Argentinian Chardonnay

Thermidor: diced lobster cooked with shallots, chervil, tarragon, vermouth, mustard and cream, piled back into the shells and sprinkled with Parmesan before being browned under the grill
Wonderful with a white Châteauneuf-du-Pape or Pouilly-Fuissé – but a New World Chardonnay is a good alternative. You may prefer to combat the rich sauce with a crisp and dry white such as a Sancerre or Pouilly-Fumé

Mullet, Grey

A coarse-fleshed fish often caught off the coast of Cornwall: delicious stuffed with fennel and mushrooms and baked whole
A Riesling or dry Muscat from Alsace or even an Anjou Rosé would suit

Mullet, Red

Smaller than grey mullet, with deep pink skin, this fish has sturdy flesh. Best with the sides slashed then brushed with olive oil, lemon juice and crushed garlic and grilled
Good with a chilled rosé from Provence, a crisp white wine like an Italian Frascati or a Cape Chenin Blanc

Barbecued: stuffed with sliced fennel
Choose a Sauvignon Blanc from California or Australia

Blackened: Creole style with lots of pepper and chilli
This calls for something that can cope with the spices, such as a very cold Sauvignon Blanc

Grilled with Chilli
It needs a wine to cut through the fairly rich flesh so try an Alsace Gewurztraminer or zesty New Zealand Sauvignon Blanc

Mussels

Baked on the half-shell with a stuffing of breadcrumbs, garlic and chopped parsley
Good with an Italian or New Zealand Chardonnay

à la Marinière: French mussel stew with white wine, garlic and cream

Perfectly matched by a Muscadet de Sèvre et Maine sur lie, a Sauvignon de St-Bris or an Aligoté, all of which have a juicy brush of acidity

Mouclade: French mussel stew made with cream and egg yolks to give a rich creamy sauce, often flavoured with pastis
A Sancerre, Bourgogne Blanc or a white St-Véran

Romanesc: cooked on the half-shell and served cold with a sauce of pimentos and garlic, Spanish style
Choose a crisp Valencian or Penedès white

Provençale: with a tomato, shallot, garlic and pepper sauce
Well matched by a fruity red like Corbières or Languedoc-Roussillon

Octopus

Stew: cooked in red wine with garlic, thyme, marjoram, tomatoes and olive oil
A full-flavoured dish which calls for a rich wine like an inky Cahors, Australian Cabernet Shiraz or a Spanish Valdepeñas

Oysters

Deep-Fried: a Chinese speciality of oysters coated in light crisp batter, deep fried and served with oyster sauce
Choose a rice wine or Soave

Florentine: shelled oysters on a bed of cooked leaf spinach topped with cheese sauce, grated cheese and grilled until bubbling
Eat these with a Tuscan or Piedmontese Chardonnay

au Gratin: served sprinkled with white wine, breadcrumbs and cheese then grilled on the half-shell
Best with a California or Australian Sauvignon Blanc

Mornay: shelled oysters poached, replaced in their shells, covered with cheese sauce and Parmesan and browned under the grill
Good with an Australian Sauvignon Semillon or Semillon Chardonnay. A crisp Trentino Alto Adige white also complements the dish well

au Naturel: with chopped shallots, vinegar or lemon and brown bread and butter
Go for a Chablis as a first choice. But Muscadet de Sèvre et Maine sur lie, Sancerre, Pouilly-Fumé or a New Zealand Sauvignon Blanc are good, too

Pike

Mousseline: fillet, white wine and cream blended into a mousse and poached. Usually served with a crayfish sauce
This sophisticated dish will show off a good white burgundy

Quenelles: light dumplings made with ground pike
An Alsace Riesling or Bourgogne Blanc is a good choice. Alternatively, look for an Australian Sauvignon Blanc

Pilchards

on Toast: a cheap and sustaining protein-packed snack. The pilchards are usually in a rich tomato sauce

35

Nothing better than a cheap and cheerful
red from the Côtes du Rhône, Côtes de
Provence, or a Valencian red

Plaice

Breadcrumbed and Deep Fried
A light dry Bergerac Blanc or Bordeaux
Blanc is a good match

Fillets: stuffed with prawns
Try an Alsace Riesling or a Tuscan Galestro
white

Grilled with herbs
Complemented by a New Zealand
Chardonnay or a white Rioja

Meunière: pan-fried with butter, lemon
juice and parsley
Try a lively northern Italian Chardonnay with
this simple dish

Poached
Chablis, or one of the new German trocken
wines

Prawns

'Butterflied' and cooked with garlic and
parsley
Try an Australian Riesling. Chilled fino sherry
is good, too

Mayonnaise
Frascati, Soave and Verdicchio are good. So
is any New World Sauvignon Blanc

Potted: peeled prawns tossed in dill
butter and packed into pots then sealed
with melted butter
Go for a chilled tangy manzanilla or fino
sherry

Sambal: from Singapore, a hot and spicy dish. Garlic, chillis, ginger and coconut milk make the Sambal sauce
Too hot and piquantly spicy for wine, so stick to lager

Sandwich: crustless brown bread with shredded iceberg lettuce and a little Marie-Rose sauce
A dry rosé is perfect

Prawns, Dublin Bay (Langoustines)

in Irish Whiskey and garlic butter
A crisp and grassy Sauvignon Blanc. Alternatively, a glass of Irish whiskey

Salad: cold with mayonnaise and lettuce
Irresistible with Chablis, an Australian Rhine Riesling or a New Zealand Sauvignon Blanc

Sautéed in garlic butter
Needs a rich white wine like a New World Chardonnay

Quenelles: see Pike

Rock Salmon

Dogfish or huss, usually served battered with chips
A Hungarian or Yugoslav Riesling complements this well – or a real ale

Rollmops: see page 31

Salmon

Fishcakes: a simple but luxurious fishcake with flaked salmon and freshly cooked mashed potato, flavoured with parsley and lemon
Calls for the crispness of a Sancerre or any dry Austrian white wine

Grilled: steaks with herbs
A delicious dish well matched by a New World full-bodied dry white wine such as an Australian or California Chardonnay. In France, a red wine such as Beaujolais is often chosen to drink with salmon

Poached whole and served cold with mayonnaise
The delicate meatiness needs a full-bodied dry white wine such as Chablis or Pouilly-Fumé

Smoked: served with lemon and black pepper
Sancerre, Pouilly-Fumé, Chablis or New Zealand Chardonnay are all good with this

Salmon Trout

Poached whole and served cold
Deserves a good white burgundy but a Portuguese Vinho Verde is an acceptable cheaper alternative

Sardines

Grilled or barbecued with garlic and parsley
A dry white Rioja from Spain will suit this well. The crispness of the wine is a good balance to the richness of the fish

Sashimi

Thinly sliced raw fish served with horseradish and soy sauce for dipping
Choose a saké or Scotch whisky

Scallops

in Black Bean Sauce
Try a Frascati or Verdicchio with this spicy, strongly flavoured dish

Queen Scallops: large scallops steamed in the shell with shallots and soy sauce
Good with a Muscadet or New Zealand Sauvignon Blanc

Steamed
Plainly cooked these are best with the crispness of Muscadet or Chablis or a Tuscan Galestro

Scampi

Deep-Fried, coated in egg and breadcrumbs
Drink a Verdicchio or a dry blush wine with these crisp nuggets

Provençale: cooked with garlic, tomatoes, herbs and white wine
Try a new-style white Rioja or Penedès

Sea Urchins

à la Marinière: cooked in dry white wine with shallots and parsley
Goes well with a Valencian dry white or a Bulgarian Sauvignon Blanc

Shrimps

Potted in butter with cayenne
This spicy snack goes well with a buttery California Chardonnay or a crisp Cape Chenin Blanc

Skate

With black butter sauce and capers
Requires a firm wine like an Australian Chardonnay

Sole, Dover and Lemon

Bonne Femme: sole fillets cooked in white wine with cream and sliced button mushrooms

A white burgundy is perfect with the Dover but an Australian Semillon Sauvignon or Semillon Chardonnay blend would suit as well. With the lemon sole, stick to an Australian Semillon Sauvignon

Colbert: whole Dover sole stuffed with breadcrumbs and herbs
Good with a dry white Graves

Goujons: strips of Dover or lemon sole fillets coated in breadcrumbs or batter and deep fried
The best choice is a Muscadet de Sèvre et Maine sur lie, but a Cape Chardonnay is also good

Grilled: served with a twist of lemon
A white Bordeaux with the lemon sole, or a classy white burgundy with the Dover

Meunière: Dover or lemon sole pan fried in butter with lemon juice and parsley
Well matched by a white Châteauneuf-du-Pape or a California Chardonnay

en Paupiettes: fillets of Dover or lemon sole rolled around a shellfish mousse and served with a rich lobster sauce
Go for a flinty Pouilly-Fumé with the Dover and a Sancerre or Pouilly-Fuissé with the lemon sole

Véronique: Dover or lemon sole poached with white wine and cream served with seedless green grapes
With Dover sole, try one of the less expensive white burgundies such as Bourgogne Blanc. The lemon sole is good with a new-style white Rioja or Penedès

Sprats

Grilled with parsley and garlic
*These call for a Bordeaux Blanc or
Valencian white*

Smoked
Enjoy these with a chilled fino sherry

Tempura

A Japanese dish of mixed fish deep
fried in batter and served with a dipping
sauce made of dashi (concentrated fish
stock)
Keep to saké or try a fino sherry

Trout, Rainbow

Baked in red wine with herbs and a little
anchovy essence
*Enjoy this with a fruity young Beaujolais like
a Fleurie or a Bulgarian Merlot. Alternatively,
choose a Chilean Cabernet Sauvignon or a
Bourgogne Passe-Tout-Grains if you can
find it*

Fried with Flaked Almonds in butter
with lemon
Choose a Chablis or Sancerre

Fried in Oatmeal
*A New Zealand Sauvignon Blanc or white
Rioja will suit. Portuguese Vinho Verde is
another good choice*

Grilled with butter
A classic dish to go with fine Chablis

Tuna

Steaks served plain grilled with garlic and
fresh herbs
*Sancerre is a good match for this, though a
lightly chilled Bardolino from Italy will also
go well*

Turbot

Dugléré: classic dish of baked turbot
with a tomato, cream and parsley sauce
*A rich dish which will take a full-bodied
Australian or California Chardonnay*

Grilled with lemon juice and parsley
butter
*Choose a Chablis or a good white burgundy
like Meursault*

Whitebait

Tiny young herring
Deep-fried and served with lemon
*Choose a white wine from Rioja, Navarra or
Valencia*

Devilled: dredged in cayenne-seasoned
flour and deep fried
Iced lager is best

PASTA, PIZZA, PULSES & RICE

Generally these dishes are uncomplicated and usually call for a similar style of wine. But pasta, traditionally the humble Italian mainstay, has become an international dish of almost infinite versatility. In many cases it will complement more than an everyday bottle.

Arroz Negro

Black rice dish from Spain with chopped squid, peppers and onion, coloured and flavoured with squid ink
Needs a full-bodied red wine like a Rioja Reserva or an Australian Shiraz

Cannelloni

Stuffed pasta tubes topped with a creamy sauce

Spinach and Ricotta
Choose a crisp Frascati with this

Veal with Tomato
Goes well with a young Chianti

Cassoulet

From the south of France, a rich stew of beans with duck or goose and pork
Calls for a red wine from the region such as Languedoc-Roussillon, Fitou or Corbières

Chilli con Carne

Hot and spicy beef mince with red kidney beans
A sturdy dish that needs a beefy red Rhône. Or choose lager

Fried Rice

Chinese speciality of rice and chopped vegetables with seafood or chicken

Any simple white wine – Soave, for example

Frijoles

Mexican dish of fried, mashed beans –
red, pink, pinto or black – with garlic
*Rather spicy so choose an inexpensive light
red wine or, better still, lager*

Gnocchi

Italian dumplings made from choux,
potato or semolina
in Melted Butter with freshly grated
Parmesan cheese
*A full taste well matched by the fruitiness of
a young Chianti*

in Tomato Sauce
Good with chilled Orvieto Seco or Galestro

Insalata di Fagioli Cannellini

White bean salad with olive oil
*Needs a Sicilian white wine: Lacryma Christi,
Orvieto Seco, Alban white, a dry rosé or
even a young Italian red*

Jambalaya

Cajun rice dish with meat or fish and
vegetables
with Chicken, smoked sausage, ham,
prawns and herbs
*Good with a California Sauvignon Blanc or
an icy beer*

with Seafood
*Flavourful dish that needs a California dry
white like Sauvignon Blanc, a white wine
blend or a lager*

Lasagne al Forno

Well loved Italian dish: pasta layers with
a rich sauce and a creamy cheese topping

As a first course, choose a white wine like
an Italian Chardonnay, Orvieto Seco or
Vernaccia di San Gimignano. For a main
course, choose a Chianti

Macaroni Cheese

Drink a crisp white Italian wine like Pinot
Grigio or Bianco di Custoza or a lighter
Italian red like Bardolino or Rosso Cònero

Nasi Goreng

Malaysian rice dish flavoured with spring
onions, tomato and chilli and topped
with an omelette
Best with lager

Noodles

with Cream Cheese

This will set off a new-wave Italian
Chardonnay or Galestro

Japanese: transparent noodles made
from mung bean paste and served with
fish and vegetables
Drink saké, dry sherry or an inexpensive
white such as Soave

with Melted Butter and black pepper

Valpolicella, Bardolino or young Chianti is
the answer to this

with Pesto Sauce: fresh basil, garlic,
pine nuts, Parmesan and olive oil
This needs an Italian or French dry rosé

Singapore: egg noodles with onions,
garlic, prawns, char sui (Chinese roast
pork) and beanshoots
Tiger beer, or any other lager, is the
quencher to serve with this, otherwise an
inexpensive white wine like Frascati or Soave

Paella

Saffron rice dish. The authentic version is a diverse mixture with rabbit, snails and lima beans
Drink a dry white or light red from Valencia with this

with Chicken, Peppers and Peas
Try a Spanish red such as an unoaked Rioja or Penedès

Seafood: popular all over Spain
Drink a dry white wine from Penedès

Pasta

It is the sauce served with the pasta that dictates the wine no matter what form the pasta takes
Aglio e Olio: olive oil, hot peppers and crushed garlic
Choose a fresh-tasting white like Galestro or Pinot Grigio

Alfredo: melted butter, freshly grated Parmesan and cream
A Vernaccia di San Gimignano or Orvieto Seco will suit this

Bolognese: minced beef, tomatoes, onions, garlic and herbs
Needs a good Chianti Classico or Montepulciano d'Abruzza

Burro e Salvia: melted butter and fresh sage
Match this with a Verdicchio

Carbonara: egg, bacon or ham and Parmesan
Rich and creamy, so choose a new-wave Italian Chardonnay

Marinara: fish and shellfish, tomato and oregano
Especially good with a Soave

Napoletana: fresh tomatoes, garlic, olive oil and basil
Bursting with taste, this is delicious with a young red like Valpolicella, Bardolino or Dolcetto d'Alba

Pesto: deep green paste of fresh basil, olive oil, garlic, pine nuts and freshly grated Parmesan
This strongly flavoured sauce calls for a Cabernet Sauvignon or Merlot from the south Tyrol

Picchi-Pacchi: anchovy fillets, olive oil, garlic and basil
Goes well with a crisp south Tyrol Riesling Italico or a Sauvignon Blanc

Primavera: melted butter, freshly grated Parmesan, cream and finely chopped vegetables
Drink a Gavi from Piedmont with this or a Sicilian white

Vongole Bianca: clams, white wine, cream and chopped parsley
Well matched with a Frascati

Vongole Rosea: clams, red wine, tomatoes and garlic
Choose a young Chianti

Pilaff

Rice cooked in stock with vegetables or meat until all the liquid is absorbed
with Chicken, onions, garlic, mushrooms and saffron

A Soave, Verdicchio or Frascati will match this well

with Mushrooms, brown rice, onions and garlic
A sturdy dish that needs one of the cru Beaujolais like Moulin à Vent

Oriental: saffron rice flavoured with coriander, ginger, turmeric and chilli with sweet peppers, garlic and sultanas
Try a spicy Gewurztraminer from Alsace or a dry Muscat

Pizza

Marinara: seafood
Needs a Frascati or Verdicchio

Napolitana: tomato and herb with mozzarella cheese
Choose a young Chianti or Valpolicella

Quattro Formaggio: four types of cheese
Go for a medium red such as Dolcetto d'Alba or Nebbiolo d'Alba

Portuguese Rice

Flavoured with bacon, onions, garlic, chilli and soy and finished with a few plump sultanas
A crisp Vinho Verde or a dry white Dão or Alentejo

Ravioli

Small pasta parcels with a savoury filling
Minced Beef: served with tomato sauce
Choose a fruity young Chianti

Porcini: with the velvet-topped wild mushrooms ceps, affectionately known in England as penny buns

Good with a Chardonnay from the south Tyrol

Spinach and Ricotta Cheese
Best with a white wine like Vernaccia di San Gimignano or Lacryma Christi or a Sicilian white

Rise e Bisi
One of Venice's famous rice dishes flavoured with parsley and nutmeg
Needs a Bianco di Custoza, Verdicchio or Frascati

Risotto
con Funghi: mushrooms
Good with a light red like Bardolino or Valpolicella

alla Marinara: with seafood
Try a Soave or Frascati

Milanese: with saffron and Parmesan cheese
Choose Galestro. Otherwise, an Australian Chardonnay

Piedmontese: with sliced white truffles, mushrooms and sweet peppers
Enjoy this with a young fruity Dolcetto d'Alba or young Chianti or, in the summer, a new-wave Piedmont Chardonnay

Vegetable
A chilled fino sherry or a crisp Soave will suit this

Wild Rice Casserole
Cooked slowly with chopped tomatoes, sweet peppers, spinach and onion
New Zealand or Chilean Chardonnay makes a good partner

POULTRY & GAME BIRDS

The range of tastes in this section runs from the comparatively light flavours of chicken and turkey to the rich intenseness of goose, duck, pigeon and game birds. The former need full-flavoured wines to lift them and the latter need such wines to act as a balance.

Chicken

Chasseur: chicken in white wine sauce with mushrooms
Try this with New World Chardonnay

Chow Mein: Chinese dish of chicken and rice
Good with Frascati or Soave

Circassian: boiled chicken with a sauce of almonds and hazelnuts
A dry Alsace Riesling or Pinot Grigio from Italy is a good match

Cordon Bleu: chicken breast filled with ham and cheese
Good with a Chablis or Sancerre

Coronation: served cold in a lightly curried mayonnaise with chopped apricots or other fruit
Needs the fresh crispness of a Vinho Verde

Enchiladas: corn tortillas softened in oil and stuffed with chicken then topped with spicy sauce and cheese
Goes well with a dry rosé or chilled lager

Fricassée: small joints with onions and mushrooms in a white wine and cream sauce
Well matched by a lively Italian Chardonnay

with Garlic: 40 cloves! A whole chicken roasted on a bed of unpeeled garlic. The garlic mellows and looses much of its pungency
A California or Australian Sauvignon Blanc is good

Kiev: breast filled with garlic and parsley butter which spills a river of fragrant sauce
Choose an Alsace Riesling, Pinot Blanc or a Bergerac Blanc

Kromeskies: minced chicken combined with chopped onions, bacon and green peppers dipped into fritter batter and deep fried
Choose a Hungarian or Yugoslav Riesling with this

with Leeks: a Welsh dish that brings out the true chicken taste
A crisp Sancerre provides a good complement

Lemon: showing the influence of the East, chicken cooked in a light lemony sauce
Good with an Australian Riesling

with Lemon and Tarragon: classic aromatic taste match with chicken
Try a white Rioja or Navarra

Liver, Chopped: A Jewish dish of chicken livers cooked with onions, garlic and chopped hard-boiled eggs
A wide range of white wines suit this including New Zealand Sauvignon Blanc, Chilean or Bulgarian Chardonnay and Cape Chenin Blanc

Marengo: chicken pieces with onion and garlic served with croûtons and fried eggs. This dish was invented by Napoleon's cook at a time when these were the only ingredients available
A Bordeaux Blanc suits this well

Maryland: American feast of deep-fried breaded joints of chicken accompanied by fried bananas, corn fritters and bacon rolls
With its odd mixture of flavours this is tricky, but a California Sauvignon Blanc is a good match

Paprika: chicken simmered in paprika-flavoured stock with soured cream
Good with a Hungarian dry white wine or Gewurztraminer

Poulet en Daube: chicken with tarragon cooked in a white wine stock in a sealed daubière
Needs a crisp New Zealand Chardonnay

Roast Chicken
Choose a good free-range chicken for this simple but delicious dish
This calls for a decent bottle of Chablis or Pouilly-Fumé. For special occasions open a good white burgundy

Satay: chicken pieces on a skewer with a peanut sauce
The spiciness of this dish is good with the bone-dry scented fruitiness of a Gewurztraminer or an Alsace dry Muscat

Stir-fry: fast-cooked strips of chicken and vegetables

*Delicately flavoured – but needs the bite of
an Alsace Riesling*

Stoved: Scottish country dish of layers
of potato, onion and chicken pieces
cooked in chicken stock and flavoured
with thyme
Try a New World Chardonnay with this

Teriyaki: cubed chicken breast fillets and
livers, marinaded in soy sauce and saké
with fresh ginger then skewered and
charcoal grilled
*Saké is a first choice, though a California
Sauvignon Blanc would suit*

Timbale: a cross between a custard and
a soufflé set in small moulds and
flavoured with chicken forcemeat
An Alsace Sylvaner or Pinot Gris is perfect

Véronique: cold poached chicken in a
creamy sauce with white grapes
*A bottle of Australian Riesling or a dry white
from Penedès is a good choice*

Wings, Arabian style: marinaded in
olive oil, lemon juice, garlic, coriander
and chilli and charcoal grilled
*A peppery Australian Shiraz stands up to
this spicy Arabian dish*

Wings, Chinese style: marinaded in
ginger, garlic, soy sauce and sesame oil,
deep fried then sprinkled with toasted
sesame seeds
Good with a dry rosé from Portugal or Spain

Curry

Biryani: mildly spiced chicken and rice
served with a separate vegetable curry

An inexpensive Australian Chardonnay. Or lager

Korma: mild creamy curry with almonds, served with pilau rice
A glass of house white wine or Vinho Verde works well. Or lager

Madras: hot and spicy
Iced water or lager

Pasanda: mild, with almonds and cream
A medium dry Anjou rosé

Tandoori: northern Indian dish of chicken joints marinaded in yogurt, coriander, cumin, chilli, ginger, garlic and lemon juice then cooked in a clay oven
Best with an iced lager but Bordeaux Blanc, Muscadet or Entre Deux Mers can be pleasant

Tikka: boneless chicken threaded on a skewer and cooked Tandoori style
Bordeaux Blanc or Muscadet are the best choices with this spicy dish

Coq au Vin

Chicken stew from Burgundy with bacon, shallots, button mushrooms and garlic cooked in red burgundy and served with croûtons
Traditionally eaten with a young burgundy. Otherwise, choose a cru Beaujolais

Duck

Aylesbury: plain roasted
Pinot Noir goes well with duck, so choose an inexpensive red burgundy or a Pinot Noir from California, Oregon or Washington State

Barbary: plain roasted. There is proportionally less fat on these ducks than on most other varieties, allowing the rich flavour of the flesh to be prominent
Choose an Australian Shiraz

with Black Cherries and Red Wine
Serve with a lightly chilled red Loire such as Sancerre or a German red

with Green Olives and Sherry: a richly sauced dish from Seville
An oaky-style white Rioja would be the perfect choice but it can be difficult to find. A dry white wine from Penedès is a good alternative

Magret de Canard: pan-fried duck breast fillets with a sherry vinegar sauce
Delicious with a good cru Beaujolais

à l'Orange: pot or plain roasted and served with an orange sauce
Try a full-flavoured California or Australian Chardonnay

Peking: delicious Chinese favourite of roast duck with a crisp skin flavoured with spices, shredded and served with strips of cucumber, spring onion and a sweet sauce rolled all together in thin pancakes
One of the few Chinese dishes that likes wine. Choose a good Sancerre or flinty Pouilly-Fumé or a crisp dry rosé from Spain

Galantine

A boned chicken or turkey with a savoury stuffing, glazed and served cold in slices

*This popular buffet dish is good with a crisp
Sancerre or perhaps a Vinho Verde from
Portugal*

Game Pie

Chunks of mixed game under a hot
water crust. The pie is served cold
with tracklements (pickles and
chutneys)
*A good dish to show off a mature petit
château claret or an Australian Cabernet
Shiraz*

Goose

Confit d'Oie: goose joints slowly
cooked then preserved in stone jars
*In southwest France this local dish is served
with the Gascon red wine Madiran.
Alternatively, try a Languedoc-Roussillon or
red Rioja*

Roast: traditional English Christmas dish
served with apple sauce, red cabbage and
chestnuts
*This dark rich meat is best with a good
young petit château claret or a mature cru
Beaujolais*

Grouse

Small, flavoursome game bird with rich
dark meat, plain roasted and usually
stuffed with fruit
*A treat which traditionally calls for a good
bottle of claret, Hermitage, Gigondas or
Châteauneuf-du-Pape from the southern
Rhône*

Guinea Fowl

Pot-Roast: in red wine on a bed of
carrots

This gamey flavoured bird appreciates a California Zinfandel, a Cape Pinotage or a new-style Italian red wine based on Cabernet Sauvignon

Roast: served with fried breadcrumbs
Calls for an Italian Barolo or an Australian Shiraz

Partridge

Braised with green cabbage and red wine
Good with a Beaune or Nuits-St-Georges

Pot-Roast: with root vegetables, herbs and stock
This flavourful dish is excellent with a good Australian Shiraz

Roast
The meat has a delicate flavour so take the opportunity to open a top-class bottle of red burgundy such as Côte de Beaune

Pheasant

Breast Fillets with whisky and marmalade sauce
Needs a red wine of relatively high acidity like a Sancerre

Casseroled with carrots, onions, garlic, leeks, celery, fresh thyme and red wine
With this take a chance to explore some of the lesser-known French reds like Bergerac Rouge, Madiran or Bandol

Pot-Roast: in stock and red wine with shallots, mushrooms and olives
Choose something like Crozes-Hermitage, Cornas or St-Joseph

Roast: served with game chips and thin gravy
The perfect excuse to open a splendid wine from the Rhône like Hermitage, Châteauneuf-du-Pape or Gigondas

Terrine: a coarse one, flavoured with garlic, juniper and bay leaves and encased in streaky bacon
Go for a chunky red like Châteauneuf-du-Pape or an Australian Shiraz

Pigeon

Pot-Roast: whole with carrots, herbs, onions and garlic in a rich stock
A Portuguese dry red or Rioja will suit this gamey dish

Roast
Choose a petit château claret

Stewed in a rich red wine gravy with mushrooms, baby onions and fresh rosemary
Barbaresco, Nebbiolo d'Alba and Penedès red are all good choices

Poussin

Braised in red wine with shallots and mushrooms
Try a cru Beaujolais like a Fleurie, Juliénas, Chénas or Brouilly

Roast with butter and herbs
White Graves is good with this

Spatchcocked (split and opened out flat, rather like 'butterflied' prawns) and grilled with lots of black pepper
Try a New Zealand Sauvignon Blanc

Quail

These little birds with a subtle, gamey taste are usually served plain roasted, wrapped in bacon and vine leaves on a croûton
A good match is the gamey taste of a good Barolo or New World Pinot Noir

Quenelles of Game

Light dumplings of ground game poached in stock and served with a sauce
Moulin à Vent or Morgon is excellent with these

Turkey

Ballottine: boned turkey stuffed with sausagemeat and diced vegetables then poached and served hot or cold
Good with a white Penedès or an Australian Semillon

Cordon Bleu: breast fillet stuffed with ham and cheese, breadcrumbed and fried
Goes well with Pouilly-Fumé or California Sauvignon Blanc

Coronation: cold turkey pieces with apples, celery and walnuts in a light curry mayonnaise
Choose an Australian or New Zealand Riesling

Turkey and Ham Pie: (cold) in a hand-raised crust
Good with a glass of Sancerre

Turkey and Ham Pie: (hot) chunks of meat in a white sauce topped with puff pastry
A Bordeaux Blanc or white Rioja suits well

Roast: the traditional Christmas dish with forcemeat and herb stuffing, served with bacon rolls, chipolatas, parsnips and sprouts
A good-tempered bird that goes well with a variety of wines including New World Chardonnay, Australian Semillon Sauvignon or, for something unusual, a good German Kabinett wine. But try a Côtes du Rhône if you prefer a red

Salad
Good with Vinho Verde

Thanksgiving: roast and served with creamed sweetcorn and pumpkin
California Chardonnay is the perfect answer

Woodcock

A small game bird, roasted whole and served on a croûton
Red burgundy or an Oregon Pinot Noir complement well

MEAT

Meat is usually classified as red or white and as a very general rule the colour of the meat matches the colour of the most appropriate wine. Red meat, say, rare roast beef can be the best excuse to drink a classic red like a fine old claret or burgundy.

Wines to choose with roasts or grills usually follow the colour guideline according to the choice of meat alone, but wines to drink with less formal dishes like stews, pies and casseroles depend very much on the other ingredients present in the dish.

Bacon

Boiled with parsley sauce
Choose an Alsace Pinot Blanc

with Cabbage: a country dish from Ireland
Alsace Riesling or Guinness

with Pease Pudding
Delicious with a bottle of English or German dry white wine

Beef

Boiled: with whole carrots, turnips and dumplings – a satisfying and flavourful English dish
Good with a New Zealand dry red or a fruity Chilean Cabernet Sauvignon

Braised: chuck steak slow cooked on vegetables
Robust and tasty, this needs to be matched with a wine which has similar characteristics. Try a red Rioja, Australian Shiraz or California Zinfandel

Brisket: braised, spiced with peppercorns and berries: a warming winter dinner
Well partnered by an inexpensive Beaujolais

Burgers: home made with freshly minced beef, herbs and seasoning, served in a bun or with chips
A Portuguese red such as Dão would be a good choice, or your favourite house red

Hash: mashed potatoes and chopped beef with carrots and onions
Choose an inexpensive red wine like Bardolino or Valpolicella

Jellied: a buffet dish, usually topside, cooked slowly in red wine with a calf's foot until meltingly tender. The liquor sets to a jelly. Served cold in slices
A red wine from Chile, New Zealand or the Cape is the best accompaniment

Roast: with Yorkshire Pudding
This is the excuse to open a good claret, an old California or Australian Cabernet, a Grange Hermitage, a top Rhône, a Vega Sicilia from Spain, a Sassicaia or Tignanello from Italy or a Château Musar from the Lebanon

Stir-Fry: with mixed vegetables
Needs the bite of an Alsace or Australian Riesling

Stroganov: fillet of beef in strips cooked with mustard and mushrooms in a soured cream sauce
The delicate flavour is well accompanied by a Hungarian red or a young red Rhône

Wellington: fillet of beef topped with mushroom duxelles, wrapped in puff pastry and baked glazed with egg
A luxury dish that calls for a mature Châteauneuf-du-Pape or Hermitage

Boeuf

à la Bourgignonne: richly flavoured stew of beef cooked in red wine with button mushrooms, lardons and shallots
Traditional dish of Burgundy so a red burgundy would be the appropriate choice, otherwise a Barolo

en Daube: beef with herbs and vegetables in red wine cooked in a sealed daubière
Good with an Australian Shiraz or an inky Cahors from France

Ragoût: lean beef cooked with mushrooms and root vegetables
A hearty dish which calls for an equally hearty wine like an Australian Shiraz, California Sauvignon, Vino Nobile di Montepulciano or the Spanish Ribero del Duero

Bollito Misto

From Italy, a selection of boiled meats served with a sauce of garlic, parsley, capers, shallots and pine kernels
This country dish needs a red wine such as a Piedmontese Nebbiolo or a Barbaresco

Boudin Blanc

French white sausage made from veal
Well matched with a Muscadet, Sancerre or a dry white Graves from Bordeaux

Brains, Calves'

in Black Butter with capers
Needs a red, perhaps a Cabernet Sauvignon from Hungary or Bulgaria

with Sauce Ravigote: a vinaigrette with chopped shallots, capers and herbs
A dry red wine from Chile or Argentina would be a good choice

Budin de Tenera

Ground veal sausages from Spain, served with tomato sauce
This rich and filling dish needs a Navarra Rosada or a young unoaked red Rioja

Châteaubriand

Double fillet steak always cooked for two, named after the eighteenth-century French writer and traditionally served with Sauce Béarnaise
Calls for a good mature claret or a Cabernet Sauvignon from California or Australia

Cholent

Jewish beef stew flavoured with paprika and garlic with root vegetables and barley. Made on Friday and cooked slowly to be ready for Saturday lunch
Try one of the new Cabernet Sauvignons from Israel or a southern French wine such as Languedoc-Roussillon or Minervois

Choucroute

From Alsace, a dish of pickled cabbage cooked with pork and sausages
Rich and satisfying, this needs an Alsace dry Muscat or Tokay. Locally, Gewurztraminer often accompanies it

Corned Beef Hash

Mashed corned beef with potatoes and tomatoes
Goes well with a California dry red blend or a Zinfandel

Cornish Pasty

Old-fashioned pies filled with diced lamb, carrot, swede and potato – originally a self-contained 'packed lunch' for Cornish miners
The miners drank thirst-quenching ale but try a simple red such as a Languedoc from France, Valencia from Spain or Bardolino from Italy

Cottage Pie

An English country dish of minced beef and onions topped with mashed potatoes
An Australian or New Zealand red blend is a good choice

Curry

Biryani: mildly spiced mutton curry and rice served with a separate vegetable dish
An inexpensive Australian Chardonnay. Or lager

Dupiaza: spicy mutton curry with plenty of onions
Dry rosé. Or lager

Korma: mild and creamy
Sip a glass of house white or a Vinho Verde. Or lager

Madras: hot and very spicy with chillies
Iced water. Or lager

Pasanda: a basic mild curry with almonds and cream
A medium-dry Anjou rosé

Rogon Josh: very spicy sauce with green peppers and tomatoes
A lightly chilled Bardolino. Or lager

Vindaloo: seriously hot and spicy
Choose a Kingfisher or other lager. No wine will survive this

Doner Kebab

Sliced marinaded lamb, slowly spit roasted
Good with a Greek or Cypriot red wine, a Spanish red Valencia or a glass of beer

Enchiladas

Mexican corn tortillas, softened in oil, stuffed with minced lamb, chicken or beans then topped with a spicy sauce and cheese
Goes well with a dry rosé or Mexican lager

Fabada Asturiana

One of Spain's best-loved dishes: beans cooked with the spicy Spanish sausage chorizo, onion, garlic, a pig's trotter and morcilla (Spanish black pudding) and served with crusty bread
Superb with a young red Rioja or a Valencian red

Faggots

A rich Scottish (and Irish) dish of pork offal minced with herbs and onions and shaped into balls
Good with a young red wine such as a Bulgarian Cabernet or Merlot

Fondue Bourgignonne
Strips of fillet steak dip cooked in hot oil and eaten with relishes
Good with a decent Beaujolais like a Fleurie or Brouilly

Frankfurters
Long thin German pork sausages, often served with mustard, sometimes in a bun as hot dogs
Best enjoyed with a beer

Frikadeller
Danish minced pork and veal patties served with tomato sauce
Good with a chilled Loire red or a dry rosé

Gammon
Boiled and served cold in slices
Delicious with a fresh fruity Beaujolais or unoaked red Rioja

Roasted with a honey and brown sugar glaze and served hot
Well balanced by a red Bordeaux or a glass of stout

Steaks: served with pineapple
Sweet and savoury flavours compete in this popular dish so choose an inexpensive house red

Goulasch
Paprika-flavoured beef or pork stew with tomatoes and onions, topped with a swirl of soured cream
This tasty dish needs a spicy wine like a peppery Australian Shiraz or a Côtes du Rhône. Alternatively, try a Hungarian red wine

Gumbo

A Cajun dish of seafood and ham cooked with tomatoes, okra, onions and garlic, flavoured with chilli sauce and served with rice
Rather too spicy for a wine: stick to lager

Haggis

Traditional Scottish dish of sheep's offal, oatmeal, onion and parsley stuffed into the stomach of a sheep and served with a glass of whisky poured over
Needs a young red wine from Bordeaux, though in Scotland it is often served with malt whisky

Ham

Bayonne: lightly smoked, from the south of France
Well matched by a light red like Bandol, Chinon or Bourgueil

Boiled: served cold with mustard
Goes well with a New Zealand or Chilean dry red wine such as a Cabernet Sauvignon

and Cheese Toasted Sandwiches
A glass of Côtes du Rhône. Or lager, ale or stout

Roast and Honey-Glazed: served hot or cold
A mixture of salt and sweet flavours, so drink a young and fruity red like a Merlot

Sandwiches, Toasted:
Be sparing with the mustard and serve these with a house claret

York: mild flavoured, lightly smoked British ham served cold

If possible pick a New World Pinot Noir, otherwise a house claret

Hamburgers

The nation's snack meal, usually served with tomato chutney and gherkins in a bun

Try a fruity red wine such as a Chilean Cabernet Sauvignon – or a Merlot from California

Hare

Jugged: A rich stew thickened with hares' blood

This robust dish needs a big red wine such as an Australian Cabernet Shiraz, Cahors, Ribero del Duero or a Sicilian red

Potted: a British dish of marinaded hare and bacon cooked with shallots and juniper berries, seasoned then packed into an earthenware dish

Well matched by something young, fresh and fruity from southern France. Try a Fitou, Corbières or Minervois

Roast: usually the saddle, cooked wrapped in bacon and served with a redcurrant sauce

Rich and tasty, this is a good foil for a decent middle-rank claret or a Brunello di Montalcino

Heart

Lamb: in most cases stuffed with onions and herbs and braised slowly in a rich gravy

This robust dish needs the full-bodied fruit of a decent Portuguese red like a Dão or a Bairrada

Ox: pot-roasted, this dish has a similar flavour to goose
Tasty with a Chilean Cabernet Sauvignon

Himmel und Erd (Heaven and Earth)

Apples from heaven and potatoes from earth – a German country dish of apples, potatoes and bacon
In Germany try a Spätburgunder, elsewhere a young Beaujolais

Huntingdon Fidget Pie

A traditional English country recipe of bacon, potatoes, apples and onions cooked in cider and topped with shortcrust pastry
Try a tankard of dry cider or a dry English wine

Irish Hotpot

Mutton, vegetables and kidneys in a white wine stock
A country dish, superb with Guinness or an inexpensive claret

Irish Stew

Traditional dish made with neck of lamb, potatoes, turnips and carrots in a mutton stock
Enhanced by an Australian or Cape dry red. Or try a glass of Guinness

Jagdwurst

German minced pork and ham sausage
Best matched with a Franconian wine or German beer

Jambon Persillé

A Burgundian speciality of ham cooked on the bone then diced and set in aspic with plenty of chopped parsley

A Bourgogne Rouge is a good accompaniment, or for something a little more up-market, try a Côte de Beaune-Villages

Kangaroo

Now a gourmet dish in Australia this has the taste of lamb and venison. Usually served with a rich wine sauce
Takes perfectly to an Australian Shiraz, but for the ultimate Australian dinner, choose the great Grange Hermitage

Keftedes

Lamb meat balls in tomato sauce
Good with Greek, Cypriot or other dry red wine

Kidneys

in Creole Sauce: tomatoes, peppers and capers flavoured with chilli and lemon juice
Go for a cooling chilled rosé from Provence with this dish

Devilled: with mustard, Worcestershire sauce and tomatoes
Rather spicy, this needs a peppery Shiraz from the Rhône or Australia

Grilled
A young but sturdy dry red wine, say an Australian or California blend, would be a good match. Alternatively, try a red Portuguese such as Dão or an Italian Montepulciano

with Onions, Garlic and Cream
Choose a fruity red wine such as an inexpensive burgundy, Beaujolais or Dolcetto d'Alba

Sautéed in a sherry sauce
Match this with a good dry oloroso

Turbigo: cooked in a rich gravy of
sherry, beef stock, tomato purée and
onions and served with croûtons
*Enjoy this with a big wine from the Rhône
such as Hermitage or Gigondas*

Kleftico

A Greek dish of a lamb shank cooked
until tender with herbs and usually
served with rice
*A robust and filling dish that needs a good
Greek or Cypriot red*

Klops

Polish meat loaf
Good with a Bulgarian Merlot

Kofta

These are spicy Indian meatballs, usually
lamb, flavoured with onion, garlic and
cinnamon and served covered in a
coconut sauce
*Spicy but creamy, these could be
accompanied by a dry Sauvignon de St-Bris
or an Aligoté from Burgundy*

Lamb

Crown Roast
*An excuse to open a mature claret or red
burgundy*

Cutlets: plain grilled
*Always good with claret, but try an
Australian or California Cabernet Sauvignon*

Flageolet: leg of lamb roasted on a
trivet with flageolet beans cooking in the
juices beneath

A robust southern French red or Cape Pinotage will match this well

Guard of Honour: intertwined best end of neck of lamb with a rice and herb stuffing
Choose a Spanish Rioja Reserva or Gran Reserva with this celebration roast

Haricot: a French provincial casserole made from inexpensive cuts of lamb stewed with haricot beans, tomatoes, garlic and herbs
A filling and comforting dish, best with a red wine from the Languedoc-Roussillon, Minervois or Corbières regions of southern France

Kebabs
Choose something gutsy like an Australian dry red

Kofta: see page 72

Noisettes: lamb fillet trimmed into rounds then pan fried and served with redcurrant sauce
A Beaujolais or young Chianti is right with this. The acidity of the wine will combat the sauce

Roast: leg or shoulder with garlic and rosemary
A classic roast and a good excuse to open a bottle of fine claret, a mature Chianti Classico or a red Rioja

Spit-Roast: smothered in olive oil, sprinkled with garlic and fresh herbs then roasted over charcoal

California Zinfandel, a young claret or red
Rioja make good partners for this fragrant
dish

Lancashire Hotpot

A famous northern English casserole of
lamb and vegetables, layered and topped
with sliced potatoes
A substantial dish well matched by a Côtes
du Rhône or Rioja Reserva

Liver

Alla Veneziana: a Venetian dish of very
thinly sliced calves' liver with heaps of
slowly cooked onion rings
Delicious eaten with a young and fruity
Bardolino

Calves': grilled and thinly sliced
This is a Pinot Noir dish

Grilled: with a sherry vinegar sauce
Try a young and fruity red Rioja or
Valpolicella

Lambs', with Bacon
Simple and tasty. Good with a light young
claret

and Onions: sliced lambs' liver with
onions and bacon, casseroled in rich
gravy
A peasant dish. The best accompaniment is
a red country wine like a Fitou or Corbières

Meat and Potato Pie

Substantial dish of chunks of tender
steak, onions and potatoes in gravy with
a shortcrust top
Serve with an inexpensive red wine from
New Zealand or Chile

Meatballs

Italian: well seasoned garlicky minced beef shaped into balls and served with a fresh herby tomato sauce
Best with a young Chianti

with Parsley: served with spinach sauce
Try a California Zinfandel with this

Merguez Sausages

From the south of France. Spicy and hot, served with mashed potato
Needs a crisp Provençal rosé or lager

Mince and Onions

An everyday dish of minced beef with onions, tomatoes and mixed herbs
A Portuguese red from the Dão, Bairrada or Alentejo regions is a good choice

Moussaka

Greek dish of layered minced lamb, aubergines, tomatoes, onions and garlic with a yogurty cheese sauce
Choose a Greek red wine for authenticity or any light young red

Mutton Pie

Layers of mutton, potato slices and kidneys with chopped tomatoes in a puff pastry case
An inexpensive Bulgarian Cabernet Sauvignon or Merlot will suit – or a dry Portuguese or New Zealand red

Navarin

Classic French stew of lamb or mutton with onions, potatoes or other root vegetables
Good with a hearty Italian Barolo or Brunello. Or a less expensive Midi red

Navarin Printanier

A version of Navarin using baby spring root vegetables such as carrots and turnips

A delicately flavoured stew, so a young claret will suit

Osso Buco

Italian stew of chopped veal shin flavoured with onions, garlic and herbs

This rich and delicious dish is complemented by a Brunello di Montalcino, Chianti Classico Riserva, a Vino Nobile di Montepulciano or an Australian Shiraz

Oxtail

Braised in Red Wine with onions, garlic and thyme

Good with an Australian Cabernet Sauvignon or Shiraz or a blend of both

in Stout or Beer

The sauce is quite sweet, so try a dry Spanish red from Navarra, Rioja or Valencia

Pork

Afelia: Greek stew of pork chunks marinaded in white wine and coriander and cooked in wine and stock

This flavourful dish is best accompanied by a Greek white wine or a light red like Beaujolais, slightly chilled

Casseroled with Prunes

This subtle mixture of fruit and meat goes well with a New Zealand or Chilean Sauvignon Blanc

with Chilli and Salt: Chinese finger food

A lager is good; so is a dry rosé

Chops with Onion Gravy
Try a young claret or Australian Cabernet blend

with Ginger and Garlic, spring onions and soy sauce
Muscadet will suit this dish

Marinaded then grilled and served with a barbecue sauce
Needs an icy lager or a red Côtes de Provence

Médaillons of tenderloin with mustard and cream
Try a bone-dry Sancerre or New Zealand or Italian Chardonnay

Normande: with apples, Calvados and cream
A big full-flavoured California or Australian Chardonnay

Roast: loin or leg with sage and onion stuffing and apple sauce
Choose a Bourgogne Rouge or a New World Pinot Noir. A light New Zealand Cabernet Sauvignon or young Chianti Classico would also go down well

Sambal: hot and spicy dish of chillis, ginger, coconut milk and chopped pork
Choose an inexpensive lightly chilled rosé or Beaujolais

Satay: from Southeast Asia: skewered strips of pork with a spicy peanut sauce
The spiciness of the sauce is good with the bone-dry but scented fruitiness of a Gewurztraminer or Alsace dry Muscat. Otherwise, lager is a refreshing choice

Sausages: flavoured with herbs and served with fried onion rings
An everyday dish, good with a Bulgarian Cabernet Sauvignon or Merlot

Sausages and Chips
The best wine to drink with this is a cheap young red such as Hungarian Bulls Blood

Sausages and Mash
Choose a Bulgarian Cabernet Sauvignon or Merlot

Spare Ribs: barbecued in a spicy tomato sauce
Good with a Provençal or Tavel rosé

Sweet and Sour: Chinese style crispy pork balls covered in a sweet and sour sauce
Goes well with a spicy Gewurztraminer or medium-sweet Portuguese rosé

Pot au Feu
Chunks of tender beef cooked with carrots, onions, celery and turnips in a rich broth
Choose a California or Australian Sauvignon Blanc

Rabbit
with Mustard: joints flavoured with Dijon mustard, cooked in stock with onions
A good match is a California Zinfandel, Cape Pinotage or a cru Beaujolais such as Moulin à Vent or Morgon

with Onions: joints cooked gently with sliced onions in butter and oil
A spirited Lirac or Tavel red is the answer

Pie: boned rabbit, ham and chopped
hard-boiled eggs in a creamy parsley
sauce topped with puff pastry
*An old-style, wood-aged white Rioja is
delicious with this. Failing that, a white
Rhône is good*

with Prunes: marinaded in red wine
with herbs and onions then cooked in
red wine and stock with prunes
*Goes well with an Australian Shiraz or Rioja
Reserva*

in **Red Wine:** cooked with onions,
mushrooms and bacon
*Delicious with a mature cru Beaujolais such
as Moulin-à-Vent or a Chianti Classico
Riserva*

Stew: the traditional East Anglian dish
of jointed rabbit cooked in a light stock
with carrots
*Choose a young inexpensive claret or
perhaps a richer California Chardonnay*

Rissoles

Patties of minced meat, fish or
vegetables, flavoured with onions, garlic
and herbs
*A simple dish enhanced by an unaged red
Rioja, a red Navarra or a Valdepeñas*

Salmagundy

An Elizabethan dish of cold meats and
cold cooked vegetables arranged on an
oval platter with hard-boiled eggs and a
dressing
A young inexpensive claret will suit

Salt Beef

Boiled with herb dumplings, served hot

*Try a young fruity Beaujolais like St-Amour,
Chénas or Chiroubles*

Sandwich: served on Rye with gherkins
*Enjoy this with an American lager or a
California dry red wine*

Saltimbocca alla Romana

Veal escalopes with Prosciutto
*Try one of the fuller Italian whites like
Tuscan Chardonnay or the unusual Greco di
Tufo from around Naples. A Sicilian white
also goes well*

Sauerbraten

Braised pickled beef from Germany
cooked with vegetables and spices
*Try a less well known German white wine
like Scheurebe, Franconia or Alsace
Gewurztraminer*

Sauerkraut

Cabbage in brine served with pork
shanks and sausage
*A stout dish that needs a trocken German
or Alsace Riesling or dry Muscat*

Schinken-Fleckerl

A Swiss noodle dish of smoked ham
with soured cream and Gruyère
cheese
*A rich and smooth combination which calls
for a German trocken or halbtrocken white
wine*

Shepherd's Pie

A substantial and comforting dish of
minced lamb and onions topped with
mashed potato
*Needs a good Côtes du Rhône or a dark
beer*

Shish Kebab
Chunks of lamb, onion, tomatoes and
sweet peppers marinaded in yogurt and
barbecued
*Try an Australian Shiraz or Shiraz Cabernet
with this*

Sosatie
A Cape dish of lamb marinaded in
tamarind or lemon juice then skewered
and grilled on an open fire or griddle
*Calls for a robust Cape red like Pinotage or
Cinsaut*

Steak
Plain grilled with lightly cooked spring
vegetables
*Perfect with claret or a good Australian or
California Cabernet Sauvignon*

Steak Diane
Originating in Australia, this is fillet steak
cooked with onions, lemon juice and
Worcestershire Sauce and flambéed in
brandy
*The best choice is a spicy Australian
Shiraz*

Steak and Kidney Pie
Packed with meaty flavour and topped
with crisp puff pastry
*This is good with an Australian Shiraz or an
inexpensive Côtes du Rhône*

Steak, Kidney and Oyster Pudding
Chunks of tender steak with kidney and
oysters in a rich, fragrant gravy sealed in
a suet crust
*Perfect with a robust Châteauneuf-du-Pape
or a red from Spain's Ribero del Duero*

81

Steak and Mustard Sandwich, Toasted

A glass of California dry red or a glass of lager suits well

Steak au Poivre

Fillet or entrecôte steak studded with crushed black peppercorns and cooked in butter. The sauce is enriched with cream and brandy

The pepperiness of this dish needs a spicy wine like a California Zinfandel, a Rhône Shiraz or a Cape Pinotage

Steak Tartare

Not for the squeamish, this is seasoned raw beef fillet served with raw egg yolk

Goes well with a cru Beaujolais, especially Morgon or Moulin-à-Vent

Sweetbreads

Cooked in a creamy sauce

Needs a dry German or Johannisburg Riesling

Tacos

Mexican snack of crisp corn pancakes filled with cooked pork strips

A Mexican lager sets these off best

T-Bone Steak

Grilled with garlic and plenty of ground black pepper

Perfect with a young claret or New World Cabernet Sauvignon

Teriyaki

A Japanese dish made with chopped beef fillet marinaded in soy sauce, saké and fresh ginger then charcoal grilled and served with slices of raw mushroom

Saké is the first choice, though Sauvignon Blanc can be a good match

Toad in the Hole

English country dish of sausages roasted in a light and crispy batter
Best with a traditional ale or a Bulgarian dry red

Tongue

Lambs' Tongue Salad: with diced vegetables
Choose an inexpensive New Zealand Cabernet Sauvignon

Ox Tongue: braised with baby onions, carrots and a fresh bouquet garni and served sliced with a sherry sauce
Choose a medium-priced Cape red like Pinotage or Cinsaut or a young California Cabernet or Zinfandel

Ox Tongue: braised with carrots and onions in red wine
Needs a chunky wine like a Côtes du Rhône, Minervois, Fitou or Languedoc-Roussillon

Ox Tongue: cold, served with ham
This dish takes a cru Beaujolais such as Fleurie or Brouilly

Tournedos Rossini

Rossini, gourmet as well as composer, created this dish. Tournedos, 'turn the back', is what waiters were inclined to do when it was served because it was an embarrassment to them. Now it is a popular luxury dish – tender fillets of beef cooked in butter, topped with foie gras and sliced truffle and served with a madiera sauce

A top Barolo or Chianti Classico Riserva is
appropriate

Tripe

à la mode de Caen: a speciality from
Normandy in which the tripe is
preserved in jelly
A youthful Beaujolais or Bardolino suits this

à la Crème: French delicacy made with
double cream, beef stock and onions
*Good with a sturdy white wine such as
Châteauneuf-du-Pape or Hermitage*

and Onions: cooked slowly in milk with
sliced onions
Needs a glass of Australian Chardonnay

Veal

Breast: stuffed, rolled and roasted
*Go for a Chilean or New Zealand
Chardonnay*

and Ham Pie
*This old-fashioned raised water-crust dish
suits a chilled ale or, even better, a young
claret*

Parmigiana: breaded escalopes with
Mozzarella cheese and tomato sauce
*Stick to a dry white wine like Frascati,
Verdicchio or Galestro*

Vitello al Limon

Veal escalopes in a lemon sauce
*A tangy dish, so go for a fruity red like a
Nebbiolo d'Alba or a rich Australian
Chardonnay*

Vitello alla Marsala

Veal escalopes in a sauce enriched with
Marsala

*Choose something red and dry like Chianti
or Rosso Cònero*

Vitello Tonnato

Veal, poached and served cold with tuna
fish sauce
*A young Chianti is a good choice or, in
summer, an Orvieto Seco*

Venison

Pasty

An old English game dish of venison and
mushrooms in puff pastry
*A Côtes du Rhône or a meaty Australian
Shiraz is perfect with this gamey meat. As
an alterative, try a California Zinfandel*

Roast Leg: served pink
*Enjoy a bottle of good mature claret with
this*

Roast Loin with Cranberries:
a Norwegian dish
*The best partner is a full-bodied
Australian, New Zealand or Cape dry red
blend*

Roast Saddle: served with soured
cream and redcurrant jelly
Try a California Cabernet Sauvignon

Roast Shoulder: stuffed with wild
mushrooms
*Go Italian – a truffle-scented Barolo is a
good choice*

Stew: marinaded then cooked with
onions, garlic, herbs and red wine
A Rioja Gran Reserva goes well with this

Stew with Juniper Berries: cooked in
red wine

Needs a big wine like a meaty Ribero del Duero from Spain, an Italian Barolo or an Australian Shiraz or Cabernet Shiraz

Wiener Schnitzel
Escalopes of veal coated in egg and breadcrumbs then fried
A Galestro or a light dry Italian white like Verdicchio is perfect

Wiener Tafelspitz
A Viennese dish. Beef boiled slowly with leeks, carrots and celery and served with fried potatoes, grated horseradish and apple
Choose an Austrian or Bulgarian dry red

VEGETABLE DISHES & SALADS

Vegetable dishes can range from light accompaniments (see Appetizers & Light Dishes, pages 6 to 15, for further suggestions) to robust affairs with distinctive flavours and textures of their own. Similarly, a salad may be little more than a colourful garnish or a diversion between courses or it may be a substantial meal in itself incorporating beans, fish, nuts eggs or pasta and served with a rich, creamy or piquant dressing. There is no easy answer to matching such variety with wine.

An increasing number of organic wines are now available. These are grown with the use of natural fertilisers and pest control techniques and contain little or no sulphur, an otherwise standard stabilising agent. For those with special reasons for modifying their diet these wines can be attractive: they are a popular choice with asthma sufferers, for example, who find the additives in other wines can have an adverse effect on their health.

Artichoke: see page 6

Aubergine

Fritters: sliced aubergines coated in seasoned flour and cooked on a griddle *Need the crispness of a Vinho Verde from Portugal*

Imam Bayaldi: hollowed aubergines with a filling of chopped aubergine flesh, tomatoes, onions and garlic, cooked in olive oil. The Imam, or Muslim Holy Man, is said to have fainted with joy when he tasted it

87

*You too could risk such sublime delight
by choosing a crisp, dry rosé wine from
Navarra*

Stuffed with a Provençal filling of
tomatoes, sweet peppers and olives
*Try a rosé from Provence, Navarra or
Valencia*

Avocado: see page 7

Broccoli Polanaise

Light dish of broccoli with chopped
hard-boiled egg
Vinho Verde from Portugal will suit this

Cauliflower

Cheese

*Choose a bottle of Vinho Verde from
Portugal*

Fritters

Coated in lightly spiced batter and deep
fried
Good with a chilled Muscadet

Champ

Potatoes and onions cooked in milk with
chives
Have a glass of stout with this Irish dish

Chatchouka

Tunisian dish of sweet peppers and
tomatoes gently stewed together. Eggs
are broken into the mixture and cooked
whole just before serving
*Good with a Gewurztraminer from Alsace or
a New Zealand Sauvignon Blanc*

Coleslaw

Shredded cabbage, apples, carrots and
onions in a light mayonnaise

Needs a simple dry white from Austria, Hungary or Yugoslavia. Or choose an inexpensive blended wine from California

Corn on the Cob

Freshly boiled and served with melted butter
Anything light and white: a new-style white Rioja or Australian Riesling for example

Courgettes

Stuffed with breadcrumbs, herbs and grated cheese and baked
A California dry white or Chenin Blanc is a good choice

Cous-Cous

Middle-Eastern dish of coarse semolina served with vegetable broth and the hot Harissa sauce
Lager or an Algerian red wine. For a white alternative, try a Gewurztraminer

Enchiladas

Corn tortillas softened in oil, stuffed with beans and topped with a spicy sauce and cheese
Choose a dry rosé

Falafel

Spicy chickpea balls from the Middle East served with tahini (sesame seed paste)
These are hot with chilli and tasty with cumin and coriander. A spicy Gewurztraminer goes well

Fassoulia

A Greek dish of beans flavoured with garlic, tomatoes and fresh herbs, served on its own or as an accompaniment to grills or roasts

Try a Greek or Cypriot red with this tasty stew

Ful Medames

Egyptian brown beans fried with garlic, parsley, olive oil, lemon juice and cumin
A robust and spicy combination needing a weighty white such as a California Chardonnay

Garlic Bread

Thickly sliced baguette spread with garlic butter, reassembled then baked in foil
A glass of house white

Gougère

French cheese-flavoured choux pastry ring or individual choux puffs
with Cheese
A dry white wine from Penedès or Valencia

with Creamed Smoked Fish
Enjoy this with a Bourgogne Blanc or an Aligoté

with Creamed Vegetables
A flavourful dish, good with a Bordeaux Blanc

Gratin Dauphinois

Layers of sliced potatoes with garlic, baked in cream
Well matched with a California or Australian Sauvignon Blanc

Gratin Savoyard

Thinly sliced potatoes layered with garlic and Gruyère cheese, cooked with a little stock
Good with a New Zealand or Cape Chardonnay

Insalata di Fagioli Cannellini

A sturdy Italian salad of white beans dressed with olive oil
Needs a Sicilian white such as Lacryma Christi, Orvieto Seco, an Alban white, a dry rosé or even a young Italian red

Insalata Mista

Mixed salad of rugola lettuce, cucumber and chopped radishes in vinaigrette
Perfect with a Verdicchio or Tyrolean white

Insalata do Pomodori e Peperoni

Tomatoes and sliced sweet peppers dressed with olive oil and vinegar
This fresh-tasting salad needs a house white or dry rosé from Spain

Latkes

Grated potato cakes with onion, shaped into patties and deep fried
Good with a fresh Valpolicella or Bardolino

Leek Pie

The Welsh national vegetable comes into its own in this delicious pie. Slices of leek in a creamy sauce inside puff pastry
A Cape Chenin Blanc suits this well, as does Vinho Verde

Marrow

Stuffed with breadcrumbs, tomatoes and herbs
A fruity wine like a California or Cape Chenin Blanc or white Penedès will complement this

Mushrooms

with Garlic: cooked in butter with chopped fresh herbs
Try a Bulgarian Chardonnay

à la Grecque

Cooked with tomatoes, garlic, onions, herbs and spices and served cold
Good with a New Zealand Chardonnay or perhaps a rosé from Anjou

Wild: stewed in stock and red wine
Choose a cru Beaujolais

Nut Roast

Loaf of finely chopped nuts and vegetables, breadcrumbs and herbs, baked and served sliced
Perhaps try an organic wine with this or a cool red Sancerre, Chinon or Bourgueil

Onions

Stuffed with rice, herbs, tomatoes and garlic and baked whole in stock
This needs something peppery like a Côtes du Rhône

Tart: a succulent combination of onions, garlic and cream in a yeast pastry case
Alsace Riesling seems a perfect match

Peperonata

Spicy casserole of sweet peppers, onions, tomatoes and garlic
Goes well with a dry Tavel or Provence rosé

Peppers, Roasted

Sweet peppers roasted then served cold with plenty of olive oil
Needs a crisp white or rosado from Rioja

Piperade

From southwest France: chopped red, green and yellow sweet peppers fried with garlic and olive oil with scrambled eggs stirred through

In summer drink a chilled rosé from Provence with this. In winter a red from Languedoc-Roussillon

Pissaladière

From the Nice region, a flavourful tart on a yeast dough base similar to pizza, topped with tomatoes, onions and anchovies
Best with a Côtes du Rhône, a red Aix-en-Provence or a Coteaux du Tricastin

Polenta

Italian speciality of cooked cornmeal mixed with Parmesan cheese and butter, cut into squares and served with sauce
Béchamel Sauce with cheese
Galestro from Tuscany is the answer to this one, or a young Chianti

Herb Sauce: basil, oregano and olive oil
This aromatic dish is good with an Orvieto Seco or Vernaccia di San Gimignano

Mushroom Sauce
A creamy taste best suited to a Soave

Tomato and Basil Sauce
Valpolicella, Bardolino or Rosso Cònero goes well

Potato Cakes

Hungarian or Yugoslav Riesling is an appropriate choice

Potatoes, Jacket

with Butter
Any colour you like so long as it's white

with Chilli Beans
Tone down the heat with an ice-cold lager

with Ratatouille
Try a young fresh but inexpensive red wine with this

with Soured Cream and Chives
good with a chilled dry rosé

Ratatouille

A stew of tomatoes, sweet peppers, aubergines and onions from the south of France
Great in summer with a chilled dry Provence rosé. In winter try a southern French red like Corbières, Languedoc-Roussillon or Minervois

Red Cabbage

With apples and onions
Choose a real ale or Pilsner beer

Rice Creole

From the Caribbean: a rice dish with sweet peppers, tomatoes, okra and chillis
Good with a lager or an inexpensive dry white wine like Bordeaux Blanc or Soave

Rosti

Swiss potato cake
Choose a white Rioja, Penedès or Bulgarian Sauvignon Blanc

Roulade

Spinach and cheese savoury roll
Especially good with a light fresh Chilean Sauvignon Blanc

Salad see also Insalata

Allemande: smoked herring, diced apples, cooked potatoes, beetroot and parsley with a vinaigrette dressing

This refreshing German salad is good with a spicy German white wine such as Scheurebe or the Hungarian Muscat Ottonel

Composée: a dressed salad of mixed ingredients including tomatoes, mushrooms, celery and spinach
The composite flavours of this dish call for a full-bodied white wine such as Chardonnay

Greek: chunky mixture of cucumber, tomato, onion, black olives and cubes of fetta cheese dressed with olive oil and vinegar
The pine-resin flavoured retsina is good with this. Alternatively, try a Greek or Cypriot dry white wine

Green: an assortment of fresh crunchy salad leaves and green vegetables such as peppers and cucumber in a light vinaigrette
A dry white wine from Alsace, one of the lighter Chardonnays or a dry Muscat

Niçoise: a mixed salad from the south of France with tomatoes, potatoes, olives, tuna, anchovies and hard-boiled eggs in a vinaigrette dressing
A robust and tasty dish, best with a well-chilled rosé from Provence or a New Zealand Chardonnay

Russian: diced potatoes, beetroot, onion and other vegetables in mayonnaise
The iron taste of beetroot dominates this dish so it needs a simple dry rosé such as Navarra or Valencia

Tabouleh: crunchy salad of cracked wheat, onions, sweet peppers, cucumber, fresh parsley, mint, garlic, olive oil and lemon juice
The perfect choice is an Alsace Muscat or Australian Chardonnay

Tzatziki: Greek salad of yogurt mixed with cucumber and garlic
A dry Greek or Cypriot white wine – or retsina if you like the resin-like taste

Waldorf: invented in the Waldorf Astoria in New York: a dish of celeriac or celery, apples and walnuts in mayonnaise
Iced mineral water is probably best with this

Sambal

Vegetable dish served with a spicy chilli sauce
House white

Samosas: see page 14

Tapenade

French black olive and caper paste flavoured with anchovies and brandy. Often served spread on hot toasted French bread or with hard-boiled eggs and a salad
The salty olive flavour makes this a potential wine-killer so go for an inexpensive dry rosé

Tarte Basquaise

Shortcrust tart with savoury egg custard, sweet red peppers, garlic and tomatoes
An interesting partner is a light chilled Loire red like Sancerre Rouge or Chinon. Or choose an unoaked Valdepeñas from Spain with its cherryish fruit

Tempura

Selection of mixed vegetables deep fried in batter and served with a dipping sauce made from dashi (concentrated fish stock) flavoured with soy sauce and saké
Stick with saké or try a fino sherry

Tostados

Deep-fried tortillas from Mexico, often topped with avocado and cheese
Needs the crispness of a Loire or New Zealand Sauvignon Blanc

Truffles, Black

From Périgord in southwest France. Walnut-sized delicacies of the fungus family served whole in pastry
A California Sauvignon Blanc will do very nicely. Or in complete contrast try a nutty, dry, almost sherry-like Hungarian Tokay

Truffles, White

From the famous town of Alba in Piedmont, this delicious fungus with its distinctive peppery flavour is grated raw into salads or onto pasta dishes
with Pasta
Fine with a Tuscan Chardonnay in summer. In winter, try a young Chianti

with Salads
One of the new Piedmontese Chardonnays, the local white Gavi or a New Zealand Chardonnay will suit

CHEESE

Cheese is well known as a great friend of wine. Conventional wisdom is to choose either a red wine or port to serve with it. One good reason for serving the cheese course before the dessert may be that red wine left from the main course can be finished with a pleasant accompaniment; but red wine is not necessarily the only choice.

Sometimes sweet wines make stunning partners to richly flavoured blue cheeses: the celebrated match between Roquefort and Sauternes is a good example. Strongly flavoured cheeses like goats' are also often best accompanied by a crisp dry white wine.

But in general the field is wide open: when it comes to selecting a wine to go with a specific cheese the choice relies as much on personal taste as on any given 'rules'.

Many dishes based on or incorporating this very versatile ingredient can be found in Appetizers & Light Dishes (pages 6 to 15), Pasta, Pizza, Pulses & Rice (pages 43 to 50) and Vegetable Dishes & Salads (pages 87 to 98), or see a more comprehensive listing in the Ingredients Index.

Brie

Beaujolais

Camembert

A red wine from southern France such as Fitou or Corbières

Cheddar

A light claret, but a mature Cheddar with a buttery texture and touch of acidity works well with a New Zealand Sauvignon Blanc

Cheese Pie
Shortcrust pastry with egg, cream and cheese filling
This dish needs a New Zealand or Chilean Chardonnay

Cheshire
A decent Australian red or even an oloroso sherry

Dolcelatte
A dry rosé from Italy or a red Lambrusco matches this

Emmental
Try a spicy Shiraz from Australia if you like red wine with cheese. Gewurztraminer is a white alternative

Fetta
A Greek red wine

Goats' Cheese
Muscadet or Sancerre. New Zealand Sauvignon Blanc is also complementary

Gorgonzola
A spicy dry Muscat from Alsace

Gruyère
A Swiss or Austrian dry white or a light red like Bardolino

Lancashire
Any dry red is suitable but a traditional ale also works well

Mature Cheddar
Claret is a good match with a nutty mature cheddar

Mozzarella
Dolcetto d'Alba

Munster
A German *trocken* white wine

Parmesan
Barolo

Roquefort
A young red wine from the south of France such as a better Côtes du Rhône. Or try a glass of Sauternes or Barsac

Stilton
Vintage or late-bottled vintage port. The sweet white Monbazillac is a good contrast

Taleggio
A mature Chianti Classico

DESSERTS

Most desserts call for sweet wine of some sort, be it a table wine or a liqueur. There are those, however, which are better complemented by something dry.

Many puddings feature that old enemy of wine, chocolate. It is notoriously difficult, though not impossible, to find a good match and sometimes a liqueur is the best choice.

Soft fruits like wine, but hard-skinned fruits, particularly the citrus variety, often fight it. As with all dishes, of course, the best wine match depends on the combination of ingredients involved.

Apple

Bavarian, Tart: light pastry with an apple filling topped with a buttery crumble
Good with a glass of German or Austrian Spätlese

Flan, French: crisp shortcrust pastry filled with sliced apple, finished with a heavy apricot glaze
Sip a Barsac or a glass of calvados with this delicious dessert

Tarte Tatin: see page 111

Pie: traditional British pudding with shortcrust or puff pastry topping
A glass of inexpensive Sauternes would be good with this

Apricot Tart

This fruity French tart calls for an apricot brandy or the Hungarian brandy, Barak Palinka

Baked Alaska

Frozen vanilla ice cream covered with
meringue and quickly baked
Asti is a good match

Banana

Baked with brown sugar and rum
Try a light and fruity Australian Riesling

Fritters: crisp toffee outside with fluffy
banana inside
A glass of Jamaica rum is a good match

Banoffee Pie

Biscuit base with rich toffee filling and
bananas
*This is very sweet. Try sipping an Australian
Muscat*

Black Forest Gâteau
(Schwarzwälder Kirschtorte)

A rich chocolate cake from Germany
with grated chocolate and black cherries
*Good with an Austrian Beerenauslese for the
sweet-toothed or, for a contrast, a German
trocken wine*

Bread and Butter Pudding

A sweet nursery pudding
Try a sweet Barsac or Bual madeira

Cassata

An Italian ice cream bombe
*Delicately flavoured, this is well
accompanied by Asti or a glass of Vin Santo
from Tuscany*

Chocolate

Cheesecake: chocolate is a tricky
ingredient to match, particularly in this
mouth-coating form

Try a glass of Grand Marnier liqueur

Ice cream: see page 105

Marquise: sophisticated terrine made with dark bitter chocolate, butter, eggs and honey, flavoured with brandy
Sip an Austrian Auslese wine with this

Mousse: a light and delicious dessert
Even more delicious with a glass of lightly sweet German Spätlese

Pudding with Chocolate Sauce
Hungarian Riesling makes a happy marriage

Roulade: see page 109

Sachertorte: see page 109

Soufflé: flavoured with Grand Marnier
Obviously Grand Marnier with this

Christmas Cake
Sip Muscat de Beaumes-de-Venise with this or a sweet Loire like Quarts de Chaume or Coteaux du Layon. Also a good excuse to open one of the wonderful Australian liqueur Muscats or Tokays

Christmas Pudding
Splash out on a Sauternes, a Malmsey madeira or a rich Hungarian Tokay

Coffee and Walnut Gâteau
Tia Maria or Kaluha liqueur will suit this

Crema Catalan
A Spanish baked custard flavoured with lemon and cinnamon and topped with caramelised sugar
Excellent with a rich oloroso sherry or the hard-to-find sweet Málaga

Crème Brûlée

From Trinity College, Cambridge, a
dessert which pretends to come from
France. Creamy baked custard topped
with crisp caramel
*Sip a Barsac, an old Tokay or a Verdelho
madeira with this*

Crème Caramel

Sits quite easily with a Loupiac

Crêpes Suzettes

Wafer-thin crêpes with an orange butter
sauce flambéed in cognac
*These are wonderful with a glass of Grand
Marnier*

Crowdie

A traditional Scottish pudding of cream,
honey and whisky topped with oatmeal
Enjoy this with a little Drambuie

Custard Tart

A crisp shortcrust case with a baked egg
custard filling flavoured with nutmeg
A decent Liebfraumilch is called for here

Fruit Salad

Exotic: with mangoes, pawpaw, melons,
pineapple and figs, marinaded in the
cherry-flavoured maraschino
Serve with Asti

Fresh: apples, pears, bananas, pineapple
and grapes soaked in sweet white wine
Try an Australian sparkling wine

Red Fruit: richly coloured dessert with
strawberries, raspberries, cherries and
blackberries marinaded in orange juice
and vodka

A difficult one: try an Austrian Riesling or cherry brandy

Gooseberry Pie

This English shortcrust pie filled with fresh gooseberries always has a hint of sharpness
Try a Sauternes or a sweet Loire white like Bonnezeaux

Ice Cream

Brown Bread: toasted, caramelised crumbs give this ice cream taste and texture
Muscat de Beaumes-de-Venise

Cassata: see page 102

Chocolate, Dark:
Serve this with a touch of the rich raisiny Pedro Ximénez sherry – as an extra indulgence, drizzle a little onto the ice cream too. Or sip a glass of Asti

Coffee
Well matched with a glass of Tia Maria or Fra Angelica liqueur

Rum and Raisin
A glass of dark rum is a good choice

Strawberry
Complemented by a glass of Eau-de-Vie de Fraise, the clear strawberry brandy from France

Vanilla
Easily matched by any liqueur you enjoy

Jalebis

An Indian sweet of batter spirals in syrup
Probably best with Indian tea

Jam Pudding

A steamed suet pudding with raspberry or apricot jam oozing over the top
Choose a simple sweet wine such as Asti or a Moscatel de Setúbal from Portugal

Junket

An old-fashioned milky pudding set with rennet
This old English nursery dessert is good with chilled pale cream sherry – but make sure it is a pale cream

Lemon

Cheesecake: a biscuit base with a light lemony filling made with cream cheese and eggs
Lemon-flavoured liqueurs do exist but they are rather rare. Try something fizzy but not too grand, such as Clairette de Die

Meringue Pie: a crisp pastry case with a creamy lemon filling topped with meringue
The strong citrus flavour goes well with a pink Cava from Spain

Mousse: a light and airy lemon dessert made with whipped cream and egg whites
Blissful with a glass of Barsac

Syllabub: an English dessert dating from Elizabethan times, originally made by milking a cow directly into a pail with sherry in it These days the recipe is cream whipped with lemon juice and zest, white wine and sugar
A delicate enough flavour to complement a glass of Sauternes

Linzertorte

A classic Austrian jam-filled tart with a rich spiced dough base
Can be enjoyed with a glass of Austrian Beerenauslese

Melon, Iced

A wedge of melon sprinkled with ginger is wonderful with the unusual King's Ginger Liqueur, first made for Edward VII by London wine merchants Berry Bros & Rudd. Otherwise try something crisp and white like Verdicchio

Mille Feuille

Crisp, paper-thin puff pastry layers with whipped cream and strawberries
A lovely foil for champagne

Nockerlin Salzburger

A famous dessert soufflé made with eggs, sugar and lemon zest and served with chocolate sauce
A light dish, good with a German Sekt or Asti

Pain Perdu

Slices of bread soaked in egg custard then fried and topped with syrup and fruit
Good with a glass of Muscat de Beaumes-de-Venise or an inexpensive fizz

Pancakes

Jam

These are rather gooey, so choose a sparkling Saumur

Lemon and Sugar: the traditional recipe
A sparkling rosé from Saumur, Spain or Italy will suit

Maple Syrup and Cream
Sip a Grand Marnier with these

Pavlova
Meringue dessert from Australia topped with whipped cream and fresh fruit
Cava is a good match or an Australian sparkling wine

Pears
Poached in Red Wine: with cinnamon and cloves
Try a glass of red Rivesaltes

Poached in White Wine: served with chocolate sauce
Liqueur Poire William

Pecan Pie
A shortcrust shell with a rich filling of corn syrup and nut halves
A California late-harvest wine suits this American pie

Profiteroles
Light choux pastry buns filled with cream and topped with thick dark chocolate sauce
A glass of Australian late-harvest Muscat will set off this luxurious dessert

Pumpkin Pie
American Thanksgiving dessert
Traditional method sparkler: champagne itself may be going a bit too far with this pudding

Queen of Puddings
A lemony baked custard, thickened with breadcrumbs then given a layer of jam and a meringue topping

Choose a Barsac or a late-harvest wine from Australia, the Cape or California

Raspberry Brûlée

A rich custard with fresh raspberries and a crackly caramel topping
The perfect choice for this is a chilled glass of clear French Eau-de-Framboise (raspberry brandy)

Rhubarb Crumble

An English country favourite
The sharpness is well complemented by Muscat de Beaumes-de-Venise

Rice à l'Imperatrice

Creamy rice with chopped crystallised fruit
Asti or a rosé Cava

Roly-Poly Pudding

A suet crust filled with jam
This sticky dessert needs a glass of Asti or a Sekt from Germany

Roulade au Chocolat

A light and airy chocolate roll doused with liqueur, served with whipped cream
Sip a Grand Marnier, an orange liqueur with has a well-documented affinity with chocolate. Or try a glass of inexpensive sparkling wine

Rum Baba

A yeast dough ring soaked in rum syrup
Really should be eaten on its own, but if you fancy a glass of something, try an inexpensive sparkling wine

Sachertorte

Rich chocolate cake

Sip an Austrian Auslese or Beerenauslese with this

Schwarzwälder Kirschtorte:
see page 102

Shoo Fly Pie
Shortcrust pastry topped with raisins, brown sugar and spices
A California botrytized wine or a Muscat de Beaumes-de-Venise will suit this pie from America's deep south

Sorbet
Champagne
A glass of medium-dry sparkling wine

Lemon
This sweet ice is delicious with a Muscat de Beaumes-de-Venise from the south of France or a sweet sparkling Saumur

Melon
A glass of Blanquette de Limoux has a similar light fruitiness

Soufflé
Chocolate
Choose an orange liqueur such as Cointreau

Lemon
The tang of citrus means this needs a sweet wine such as a late-harvest Muscat from Australia

Nockerlin Salzburger: see page 107

Orange
Loupiac or an apricot brandy is be a good match for this

Passion Fruit: *a light dessert flavoured with tangy passion fruit purée*

Enhanced by a glass or two of inexpensive Australian fizz

Strawberries

and Cream
A luxurious dessert, best enjoyed with champagne

Fool
Choose a sweet wine to go with this: Asti or a pink Lambrusco

Gâteau: *light sponge filled with whipped cream and fresh strawberries*
A fruity Australian Riesling

Tart
A Barsac a or German Auslese suits this tart very well

Tarte Tatin

Upside-down apple tart cooked so that the apples caramelise on the bottom. Upturned before serving
Try calvados with this

Treacle Tart

An old English favourite made with golden syrup, breadcrumbs and soured cream in a shortcrust pastry case
Try Sercial or Verdelho madeira or a fine old oloroso sherry

Trifle

Banana
Try a glass of Loupiac with this addictive combination

Black Cherry with Cherry Liqueur
Sip a little Maraschino liqueur or sparkling Saumur with this

Sherry: a heavy, sweet concoction with sponge soaked in sherry in the base, a layer of fruit then custard topped with whipped cream
The Spanish fizz, Cava, is perfect with this

Upside-Down Cake

A sponge dessert made with fresh pineapple at the bottom, turned out so that the fruit is on top
With this try a glass of inexpensive fizz

Vacherin

Twice-baked meringue filled with fruit and cream
A light Barsac or sparkling Saumur is a pleasant accompaniment

SPECIAL OCCASIONS

Organising the food and drink for a special occasion such as a birthday celebration is no easy task. Even once the menu has been finalised the next problem – choosing the drinks – can still be far from simple.

If a caterer has been engaged to provide the food and wine, check the drinks with just as much care as you would the food and insist on tasting samples before finalising your choice.

If you are catering yourself, you will need to gauge how much wine you should order. If there are over, say, a couple of dozen guests you might consider making a so-called 'sale or return' arrangement with your supplier (most high street chains now offer this service) in which case any unopened bottles or cases can be returned after the event. With this arrangement you are insured against the embarrassing possibility of running out of drink in mid-party, but you do not have to be left with cases and cases of the party staple to drink your way through over the following weeks.

If you do take the prudent measure of ordering on the generous side, it can be a good idea to put some of your reserve stocks just out of the way – a drinks table positively groaning with alcohol might suggest the wrong message to some enthusiastic guests.

Normally half a bottle per person is a good rule of thumb but a whole bottle is probably a safer estimate as it ensures you will not run short. Take care to provide generously also for those who will not be drinking alcohol. Supply a good proportion of mineral water and fruit juices – especially if the weather is warm or there is dancing, for example, when everyone will be looking for something soft and thirst-quenching to drink at some stage during the party.

Special occasions usually involve speeches and toasts – and this is where many would say there is no substitute for champagne. But there are plenty of attractive sparkling wines, often made in exactly the same way as champagne, that might match the occasion just as well. Cava from Spain is one good example, or the quality sparkling wines now coming from Australia, many of which are also excellent value for money. In some instances, a daughter's engagement or the birth of a baby, pink champagne, or a pink sparkler from the Loire, Spain or Australia might lend a little light-hearted style, as well as being an attractive focal point.

If a cold buffet is involved where guests are to help themselves, it is a good idea to use a separate table for the drinks preferably in a different part of the room or party area, so that traffic to and from the tables can avoid colliding.

Choosing the wines to serve with a mixed buffet cannot, by its very nature, be an exact science. If you have provided a varied selection of food to appeal to the differing tastes of your guests, there is no way you can anticipate the combination of dishes they will select and their preferences for red, white, sweet or dry wines.

Happily, then, the choice is yours. Provide a selection of red and white wines and use the first few chapters of the book for inspiration if you need somewhere to begin. Then take full advantage of your buying power and taste as many alternatives as you can before you make a final decision. Some supermarket chains and many off-licences arrange regular tastings, others are happy to open bottles in the shop for you to sample if your order is to be of a respectable size. (It may be worth looking into whether or not your supplier hires out glasses: it can simplify the logistics if both the drink and the glasses come from the same place.)

The wines for a sit-down dinner party will depend on the menu: suggestions for each course can be found in the previous pages. The best general advice must be that whatever the scale of the gathering, it is always best to keep the food simple. As for the drink: good food and good friends to celebrate a special occasion must mean it is time to enjoy the very best wines you can afford.

PICNICS & BARBECUES

The food of the warmer months tends to be light. Fresh salads and fruits play a major role and meat and fish is simply cooked. If the weather is kind, meals can be enjoyed outside at picnics or barbecues.

Barbecues can be used to cook almost anything. Sizzling steaks, chops, kebabs and sausages are guaranteed to fill the air with mouth-watering aromas: roasted peppers, tomatoes and onions, or herb-stuffed trout make spectacular but equally simple meals.

There are plenty of speciality sausages available in good butchers and supermarkets. In summer months enterprising stores will sell marinaded meats ready for the grill: lamb cutlets in mint or rosemary and garlic; pork in sweet and sour, tandoori chicken and even ready made barbecue sauces – smoky tomato and garlic.

More variety can be added with marinaded chicken pieces, satay sticks, prawns with garlic, colourful chunks of fresh vegetables threaded on a skewer. . . indeed almost any ingredient that takes your fancy.

But barbecues are probably not the perfect time to start opening your best bottles of wine – though this might be the case if the same dishes were to be served at a formal table. Chilled crisp whites and soft, young and fruity reds (which benefit from light chilling) are the order of the day.

Summer also means picnics: fresh crusty bread, cheeses, fat black olives, cold meats and pies, crisp salads, fresh prawns – even lobster or crab are ideal candidates for the picnic hamper. Fresh fruit or glazed fruit tarts are a tempting and convenient way to round off an al fresco meal.

White wines are always a good choice with these kinds of foods, but unless a cool stream is handy, a cold box might be necessary to keep them chilled. Fruity young reds along the lines of Beaujolais are excellent picnic wines too.

If you choose fresh soft fruits for the picnic dessert, remember to take along a bottle of sweet white wine. Sauternes and, to a lesser extent, Barsac are the great sweet white wines of France – but perhaps they are a little grand for a picnic. The Loire has some fine sweet wines like Vouvray and Coteaux du Layon. Muscat de Beaumes-de-Venise from the Rhône has become fashionable, and from the Midi come the equally acceptable Muscat de Rivesaltes and Banyuls.

When it comes to summer eating outdoors, the only rules are to make it fresh and to keep it simple.

WINTER PARTIES

Winter parties for most people are centred around the Christmas and New Year festivities. If nothing else, this is when young and old make time to get together, traditionally to eat, drink and be merry.

Pre-Christmas parties are usually light-hearted affairs when the food is given less emphasis than the drink. Refreshments are often of the snack or canapé variety, and numbers to be catered for are often quite large. Wines for these occasions should be kept simple and inexpensive. A sparkling wine such as an Australian fizz, or Cava from Spain fits this bill – it also has the cork-popping razzmatazz of champagne to add to the feeling of a once-a-year celebration.

On Christmas Day itself, champagne is the obvious choice to start off the day as presents are unwrapped. But there are plenty of great value alternatives from the rest of the world, often at half the price.

Another way to start the day is with a 'champagne cocktail', such as Buck's Fizz: roughly half and half sparkling wine and freshly squeezed orange juice. Black Velvet, half sparkling wine and half Guinness, served chilled from a jug, is an alternative combination but this requires a slightly stronger constitution if it is to be attempted before breakfast. Another is the pretty Kir Royale, sparkling wine lifted with a dash of Cassis, a purpley sweet blackcurrant liqueur.

For many households, the Christmas meal itself centres on turkey, although goose, game and even large beef joints make welcome changes.

Turkey is a versatile bird (see pages 59 to 60) which takes happily to red, white and rosé wines. The final choice of wine may depend upon the stuffing and trimmings, traditionally bacon rolls, chipolatas and sauces, so these should be taken into consideration. Usually, though, an Australian or California Chardonnay is a good choice, or a red full-bodied Rhône to accompany sturdier sauces.

Richly flavoured birds like goose or duck, or game such as pheasant, need full-bodied reds to match their up-front flavours. See pages 59 to 60.

A cheese course, such as Stilton or Roquefort would traditionally be served with port: vintage if possible, or else a tawny. One of the sweeter madeiras such as Bual or Malmsey or an old oloroso sherry would be an attractive alternative

When it comes to the dessert, unequivocally pudding in this instance, a sweet wine is often called for. The richness of this dark fruity confection however sometimes works best with a glass of fortified wine or of whichever spirit is in the pudding itself. For a real treat, serve an Australian liqueur Muscat.

THE WINE GRAPES

Red Wines

Cabernet Sauvignon

The king of red grape varieties, used as the principal grape in clarets and on its own in many New World and European reds. The best clarets need years to evolve but then give marvellous cedary wines with complex flavours.

New World Cabernets are generally made to be drunk young but can also evolve. Their aroma can seem dusty and have touches of vanilla, tar, leather, pepper, spices and mulberry. The flavours show blackcurrant and oak spice and can range from dry to softly fruity.

Gamay

The grape of the Beaujolais region which gives lively, fruity, upfront wines. Though not fashionable outside Beaujolais, when the wine often becomes too thin and acid, it can be relied upon on its home patch to produce uncomplicated wines for early drinking with very little intervention.

Merlot

The lusciousness of Merlot is often used to soften the more austere Cabernet Sauvignon in Bordeaux red blends. It is adaptable and planted widely in Europe, eastern Europe and the New World.
A young Merlot typically has a whiff of blackboard chalk over a slightly sweet aroma. The flavour is plump, rich and plummy, rounded and slightly sweet.

Pinot Noir

After Cabernet Sauvignon, this is the other classic red grape variety: the one used to make red burgundies.

Pinot Noir has had mixed success in the New World. Its quality can range widely. It can suggest an extraordinary range of flavours from violets to rotting vegetables and aromas can include cherries, briar wood earthiness, raspberries, and truffles.

In red wine it is noticeably lighter-flavoured than Cabernet and has a dryish, earthy character and touches of spice.

Sangiovese

This is the Tuscan grape used to make Chianti. The best have scents of violets and many detect something earthy in its flavour but this, and indeed its quality, can vary enormously.

Syrah

Also known as Shiraz and Hermitage, this grape produces such prestigious wines as Hermitage and Côte Rotie. Although it is potentially a top quality variety there is comparatively little of it planted.

Syrah is responsible for the big peppery red wines of the Rhône Valley. It has become fashionable in California and is widely planted in Australia, where it makes rich, earthy, peppery wines.

Tempranillo

The classic Spanish red variety that forms the basis of Rioja. Unblended, it is relatively characterless, but fortified, often with Cabernet Sauvignon, its wines have a

WHICH WINE WHICH FOOD

characteristic cigar-box aroma and full, firm bramble and damson flavours.

Zinfandel

This is the native Californian variety which produces a wide range of styles. Some of its best are the dry, bright red wines, relatively high in alcohol and full of brambly fruit flavours that can develop into big, chewy reds of complexity and structure. A hint of iron filings is often detectable on the aroma.

Nebbiolo

The classic variety of the Alban Hills in Italy where it gives deep, not fruity but complex wines, often with fragrances of mushrooms. Nebbiolo wines can be long-lived but, despite top-quality potential, the vines are not cultivated seriously outside Italy.

Pinotage

A South African cross between Hermitage and Pinot. When young the wine has a lively, fruity flavour but as it matures more earthy Pinot Noir characters emerge.

White Wines

Chardonnay

The most renowned of the white varieties. It yields a spectrum of wines from the steely styles of Chablis in France to the tropical fruit aromas and lush fruity palates of many Australian versions. It is found in all the New World wine-producing countries: in California it is the first choice of growers and consumers alike.

Chenin Blanc

In the heart of the Loire Valley Chenin Blanc is used to make crisp, light and fresh whites and rich, honeyed wines such as Vouvray. In South Africa, California and Australia, the warmer weather adds light melon, fig and guava touches. Chenin Blanc makes an easy, undemanding wine with a light charm.

Gewurztraminer

An unusual grape variety which gives strong spicy aromas and flavours to an overall dry palate. New World producers have achieved patchy success with it. The grape has also been used to make sweet wines.

Muscat

There are several members of the Muscat family, most of which have been used to make wines with rich, floral, sweet aromas and a flavour reminiscent of ripe table grapes. Successful dry wines have been made from it as well as fortified wines in Australia, where its aroma is redolent of raisins.

Riesling

The true Riesling is the Rhine Riesling which forms the basis for the classic wines of Germany, ranging from dry to very sweet. A typical German Riesling has a light floral aroma and gentle fruity flavour. The best examples have the ability to age for considerable periods, when they become increasingly honeyed. In spite of Riesling's potential to produce the finest wines in the world, the variety is not cultivated in France outside Alsace. It travels fairly well and is versatile but keeps some elements of its identity wherever it goes. It is widely grown in Australia where it produces crisp, fresh wines with green apple suggestions on both nose and palate. These wines can age well, too.

Sauvignon Blanc

This is used to make two of the classic Loire wines, Sancerre and Pouilly-Fumé, two very fresh, dry and zesty wines with flinty flavours. It has also been combined with Semillon to make dry white Bordeaux wines and Sauternes, the classic sweet white wine. New Zealand has produced wonderfully bracing, mouth-watering examples which have touches of new-mown grass, asparagus and gooseberry on the aroma.

Semillon

This wine is the other half of dry white Bordeaux and Sauternes. It is also found in South Africa and New Zealand. In Australia's Hunter Valley, probably the best stand-alone Semillons are found: wines that are lemony and fresh when young but over the years develop wonderful honeyed, nutty aromas and rich delicately honeyed flavours. From the other side of the continent in the Margaret River, Semillons have herbaceous aromas which can be confused with those of Sauvignon Blanc.

INDEX OF WINES

129

INDEX OF DISHES & INGREDIENTS